BOYS

LEADER'S
MANUAL

CHRISTIAN
SERVICE

BRIGADE

CHRISTIAN SERVICE BRIGADE

Boys for Christ

OFFICIAL MANUAL

for LEADERS in

CHRISTIAN SERVICE BRIGADE

Edited by
JOSEPH WELTER COUGHLIN
and
WERNER C. GRAENDORF

CHRISTIAN SERVICE BRIGADE
542 So. Dearborn St., Chicago 5, Illinois

Board of Directors

iii

Dedication

GRAFTON B. HARPELL

New England Director, C. S. B., 1944-46

1915 — 1946

This book for leaders of boys is dedicated to the memory of one who was above all else a leader of boys.

May the work of his fellow staff members on this book reflect his thoroughness and zeal.

May the leaders who use this book follow his example of deep love for boys and devotion to the task of winning them for Christ.

May boys, like the many who knew him as "Cap," be reached for Christ through this book as he would have liked to have continued to reach them.

Table of Contents

About this book . . .

This manual was written to give you, as a Brigade leader, the necessary equipment for doing a successful job with boys.

It is well to remember that working with boys is not a mechanical
job. You are taking on the responsibility of dealing with eternal souls
and shaping lives that are plastic. Read these pages prayerfully.

The basis of the manual is the Brigade program as presented in the
BOY'S GUIDEBOOK and STOCKADER'S LOG. That program is
here interpreted and applied.

Into the compilation of the material there has gone the earnest prayer
and diligent work of the Brigade staff. Their object has been to make
this book practical, simple, and complete.

It is sent forth now with the fervent prayer that God would raise up a
host of Christian men to guide the boys of this generation into paths of
life and service for Christ.

May you, as one of these men, find great satisfaction and much fruit
in reading and applying BOYS FOR CHRIST.

Jack and Dan live on the same street.

Jack's a good sort of chap. Like most of the other million six-teen-year-old boys in America, he likes to laugh, gab around with the gang, and play his head off in sports. His pals consider him an "O.K." guy. He gets by in school — better in physics, worse in Latin. His after-school job at the corner grocery keeps him supplied with "coke" funds.

But something's missing. Jack has felt it at times, and it's bothered him. Actually, the diagnosis is simple — and crucial. Jack needs the Lord Jesus Christ. Needs him as a Saviour. Needs him as the Pilot of his ship of life. Needs him now.

Dan accepted Christ a month ago. He's fourteen. Dan's been awfully happy in Christ, and he's bubbling over with desire to do something about it. That is, he was until yesterday. For yesterday Dan's enthusiasm got sort of tired of waiting. He had some questions, but nobody answered them. He wanted to live as a Christian, but the gang just laughed. Dan needs a guide. He desperately needs someone to help him grow as a Christian He needs Christian fellowship and training that will prepare him for the challenge of Christian living. He needs it now.

The Jack and Dan of *your* street are the challenge of the fol-lowing pages.

Joseph B. Buber

General Director

BIRD'S-EYE VIEW OF

Christian Service Brigade is a Christ-centered boys' club organization, which provides a well-rounded program for boys 8 to 18. It becomes the local church's own boys' club, under the sponsorship of the church and the supervision of a church committee. Brigade is a national organization and each local group meets a definite set of standards.

History. The beginnings of Brigade go back to 1937. From its origination as Christian Service Squad, it developed into the present work, which was chartered in 1940. A number of young men, peculiarly qualified for boys' work, have merged their talents into the development of the Brigade program.

Name. The name, Christian Service Brigade, identifies the work as being *Christian*; having as its objective not only salvation, but training of boys for *Service*; and being basically a gang working together — a *Brigade*.

Beliefs. Brigade stands for the fundamentals of the Christian faith and the truth and authority of the Scriptures. It will work with any church that believes similarly.

Support. Brigade is not supported or underwritten by any one church, denomination, or organization. Its work as a missionary organization to boys is supported primarily by men who as "Brigade Dads" give regularly for its continuation. Other financial help is provided by the varying gifts of individuals and groups interested in the work.

Battalion. This is the name of the individual, Brigade-chartered club of the local church, which meets each week. Its size may vary from 10 to 40. It is for boys 12 to 18. The Battalion is broken up into smaller groups called *Squads*.

Stockade. This is the local club for the younger fellows, 8 to 11. It is entirely separate from the Battalion, having its

CHRISTIAN SERVICE BRIGADE

own program, adapted for the younger group. It is organized after a Battalion is already established.

Achievement. A key part of the Brigade program is the system of progressive ranks obtained by passing of required tests. In the course of achieving these ranks, the boy develops spiritually, physically, mentally, and socially.

Captain. The leader of the club is called Captain. He is a Christian man from the local community, above 21 years in age, commissioned from Brigade Headquarters. His co-worker is the Lieutenant.

Meetings. The Battalion meets weekly on a night set by the local group. The meeting itself consists of Squad meetings with progress in Achievement; games; devotional; and special features.

Camping. Camping holds a large place in the Brigade program. Regular camp season is planned in the summer and year-round camping is included in the total program.

Guidebook. The BOY'S GUIDEBOOK is the boy's own book which explains the Brigade program. It describes the Achievement ranks, crafts, and in general, what the boy can expect as a member of Brigade. It is for the 12 to 18 age boy.

Log. The STOCKADER'S LOG is the guidebook for the younger fellows, 8 to 11.

Boys for Christ. This is the Brigade Leader's Manual. It provides the leader (Captain) with all the essential material and background he needs to lead his local club.

Pioneer Girls. Sister organization to Brigade, Pioneer Girls have a full program for girls. (For information write their headquarters at 5334 W. Addison, Chicago 41, Ill.)

CHAPTER OUTLINE

WHY BE INTERESTED IN BOYS?

A leader is interested in boys because of their need.
A leader is interested in boys because of their great poten-
tialities.
A leader is interested in boys because of his responsibility
toward them.

THINGS EACH LEADER SHOULD KNOW ABOUT BOYS

The purpose of boyhood.
Characteristics of boyhood.
The process of growing.
    CHILDHOOD 8-12 (STOCKADE AGE)
    EARLY ADOLESCENCE 12-15 (PIONEER TRAILS AGE)
    MIDDLE ADOLESCENCE 15-18 (ADVANCED TRAILS
    AGE)

CHAPTER ONE

Boys

WHY BE INTERESTED IN BOYS?

Every leader of boys has an answer to that question, or he wouldn't be a leader of boys. For it is a man's personal interest in fellows like Jack and Dan that brings him into a boys' work. There are three main points of interest for the Christian leader.

A leader is interested in boys because of their need.

The need of boys must be met while they are boys, and their needs are real, and, primarily, two-fold.

Boys need CHRIST first of all. Every boy as an individual needs Him, for each is lost without the salvation Christ alone can provide. And boys today as a class need Christ in a greater way than ever before, for boy delinquency, as part of juvenile delinquency, remains a major national problem. But even outside of delinquency, the typical adolescent of today is commonly and realistically pictured as dissatisfied, unsettled, and seeking false excitement. Only Christ can fill the heart need and give him sure foundation and satisfaction.

Then, the second need of boys is for TRAINING IN CHRISTIAN LIVING. After the boy has been won to Christ the job is not over. It's just beginning for now the boy needs the leadership, the counsel, the opportunity that will make his life count.

Leadership — with all the force of boy-energy, fellows will follow dynamic man-leadership wherever it goes, provided it *goes*. If the right leadership is lacking in strength and virility, there will always be the wrong leadership to take its place. Today on our street corners and in our pool halls and the like there are many Pied Pipers ready to play a tune of action and adventure and of things unknown to lead boys astray. And they will eagerly follow if there is no counter-leadership. Our boys must have the vital, challenging leadership of Christian men.

Counsel — wise counsel, needed by every boy, is usually available, but seldom wanted. The guidance that a fellow will accept is that which comes from a man for whom he has respect and in whom he has confidence. Such a man is in position to help him greatly in his thinking, in his spiritual growth, and in life decisions.

Opportunity — opportunity is needed by fellows for activity and fellowship (which they will get one way or another) directed toward rather than away from living for Christ. They need opportunity, too, for service. Boys are crusaders at heart. They look for outlets for their developing abilities, and appreciate opportunities for genuine service that will really count. The Christian leader can present to boys unexcelled opportunities for service.

A leader is interested in boys because of their great potentialities.

This may be interpreted first in terms of the local church and its needs. The church's greatest human need and one of boyhood's greatest future abilities are the same — leadership.

The period of boyhood itself is a training time for manhood. A boy's normal experiences of schooling, experimentation, and the building of physical and mental strength all look ahead to the future.

The great potential that boyhood represents, when captured for Christ, can be channeled into leadership in the church — both at home and to the ends of the earth; and into Christian leadership in business, industrial, and civic life.

A leader is interested in boys because of his responsibility toward them.

As a Christian man, possibly a father with boys of his own, the boys' leader has a job to do as a man — a responsibility concerning boys' needs. From him a fellow should be able to get spiritual guidance and help in living and growing. Because so many millions of boys, even in a Christian country, cannot get that kind of help from their own dads, it falls upon individual Christian men to prepare in heart and mind to do a "dad's job" for boys.

THINGS EACH LEADER SHOULD KNOW ABOUT BOYS

The purpose of boyhood.

Growing to maturity is a business — the business of boyhood. Between the ages of eight and eighteen the boy is exposed to a required course in learning to live as a man. Some fail the course dismally and reach manhood in hardly more than the physical sense; others pass with honors, making much of their boyhood.

The decade of a boy's life between the ages of eight and eighteen is a time when he is subject to great change in physical, mental, and often spiritual development. The boy of each year is vitally and significantly different from what he was the year before. His characteristic interests suffer such violent and sometimes sudden changes, that he is often regarded as totally unpredictable. When seen in the light of the purpose and design of boyhood, however, the changes can readily be understood as typical of the boy's growth.

Characteristics of boyhood.

Despite the multitude of changes through which a boy goes as he reaches adolescence and develops toward manhood, there are significant characteristics that all boys have in common. Boys are not grown-up babies, nor are they little men — boy nature as such is distinct and full in itself.

Three basic drives of boyhood can be laid down as true of all boys of all ages. The first is his urge to BE; the second is his urge to DO; the third is his urge to LEARN. Let's examine each in turn.

First, EVERY BOY WANTS TO BE TOP-NOTCH. Basically, a boy wants to live up to his ideal of a "top-notcher." What his ideal is, of course, depends very largely upon the public opinion with which he finds himself surrounded. What a fellow reads, the gang he runs with, the men who take an interest in him, the ideals of his own parents and teachers and leaders all have tremendous effect on what that boy's ideals are going to be. Every boy — and this is especially true of adolescent boys — is undergoing a struggle for self-confidence. He wants to feel that he is "doing O.K." And he gains self-confidence, naturally, by feeling he is living up to the standards of excellence in which he himself believes.

The opinion of the gang — the fellows the boy likes most to be with and whose opinion he most respects — is an equally important force for molding his own character and decisions. Every fellow likes to be popular, and that of course means being top-notch in the eyes of the gang.

Anyone who will challenge a boy's ego by suggesting something that is hard to do, be it good or bad, is presenting that boy with a dare to prove himself proficient in that particular thing. It is boy nature to take the dare. The innocent words "I dare you to try it" are probably responsible for the destruction of more street lamps, windows, hay stacks, and high silk hats than can ever be charged to malice aforethought!

Thus, the standard of excellence set up before a boy by his leader can be one that every boy will want to strive for, provided he has real confidence in his leader. An added factor is the boy's desire, in turn, for the leader's confidence in him. Any man willing to show real interest in boys can have a profound influence upon them by the simple method of setting up standards both by life and by instruction of what it is to be top-notch.

Second, EVERY BOY LOVES ACTION. The urge to do is boyhood personified. All of a boy's developing abilities must be given some sort of outlet, and boys, naturally impatient, want action *now*. All of a boy's thinking and living are geared to the present. Even his fondest dreams are interpreted in terms of "right now."

Invite a boy, any boy on the street or anywhere, to come out to a club meeting or to some other kind of a program for boys, and inevitably his first question is, "What do you do?"

Actual physical action comes first. Boys want to be doing. They want to be having opportunities to prove their strength and to prove themselves stronger than the next fellow. Out of this emerges a boy's love for warfare, and his natural bent for fighting. Play as such has been called the most basic of all boy instincts.

Boys love competitive action. A combining of the desire for action with the desire to prove themselves tops results in the natural liking boys have to compete with one another individually and in team work.

Boys want action that is going somewhere, that is planned in its results toward definite objectives. They love to work, provided that the work produces results that they can see and appreciate.

Third, BOYS WANT TO LEARN. This cannot be safely interpreted to say boys love to study, for that is not necessarily true! But the normal curiosity, so characteristic of boyhood, is the boy's desire to learn more and more of what goes on about him. Boys of every age are continually experimenting, investigating, asking questions, trying to figure things out. And when a boy's curiosity is really aroused concerning something, he will study it endlessly and will get real enjoyment and value from it, provided his investigations are directed along the right channel.

With these three basic characteristics set forth as covering boys of all ages, the further study of boys requires an understanding of the stages of development through which a boy passes as he grows. So, serious thought should be given to the actual process of growing.

The Process of Growing.

The term *boyhood* is used in this writing in the general sense of the period of growth from infancy to manhood, not in the more specific sense which distinguishes it from adolescence.

Boyhood, thus defined, can be separated into these divisions: pre-adolescence, or childhood, including boys eight to twelve; early adolescence, boys twelve to fifteen; and middle adolescence, covering the ages from fifteen to eighteen. A later adolescent period is beyond the direct sphere of the Brigade program for boys.

In the Brigade program the pre-adolescence group is termed "Stockade Age" because of the specialized program built for these boys. The early adolescent boys work on their "Pioneer Trails." And the older boys enter upon the "Advanced Trails." We consider now some of the outstanding characteristics of each group as they effect the leader in Brigade.

CHILDHOOD 8 - 12   (STOCKADE AGE)

A boy of eight is just getting into real boyhood. He is going through a time of change. Physically the eighth year is apt to be a rather weak and sickly one. The boy of eight is taller than he was at seven, but not a whole lot stronger and not nearly as strong as he will be at nine.

His most natural instinct is play. This play instinct — a basic one with all boys — develops in distinct stages as a boy grows up. As a baby, he played by himself — throwing things, shaking things, putting things in his mouth. All of these activities were experimental in nature and neither required thinking nor involved anyone else. Now, at eight, he is still experimenting and discovering things, but he has begun to awaken to self-consciousness and to awareness of others. He is in a period of very rapid learning; his imagination is most vivid. He loves to imitate, and learns by imitating the actions of others. His social consciousness is just beginning to develop.

At ten, the boy is typically sturdiness itself. Much stronger than he was at eight, he is filled to overflowing with energy. He hasn't started to increase greatly in height and so his energy is not yet expended in growing taller. In a few years he will hit another fast growing spell in early adolescence that will again sap his energy. Now in the mid-stage, he is intensely healthy and charged with vim and enthusiasm. He wants plenty of action and plenty of noise.

This period between eight and twelve is called "Stockade Age" in Brigade; and the Brigade Stockade program is built for the interests, needs, and abilities of boys of this age. Taking the period as a unit, seven distinct principles help to understand the nature and needs of these pre-adolescent boys.

1. In the pre-adolescent boy play instincts are individualistic. Although he is becoming increasingly aware of others, he still is essentially selfish in his activities. He likes best those games which involve individual competition rather than team rivalry. His team loyalty instincts are as yet undeveloped. When boys of this age do play athletic team games they are weak on teamwork, each player playing for himself for his own glory rather than the success of the team. The "grandstand ing" and "hogging the ball" on the part of older fellows are evidences o immaturity — throw-backs to the pre-adolescent stage.

2. Boys of this early age love to dramatize, their whole bodie entering into their thinking. "Charades" and various forms of actiol

games as well as marching choruses and the like are effective for use with this age group.

3. It is a period of development in physical stamina, sandwiched between two periods of rapid physical growth. Taking full advantage of this factor requires a balanced program of exercise and athletics.

4. Because the Stockader Age boy's mental processes are also in the state of change and development, his mental ability is outstanding for two things: strength of retention in memorization, and shortness of attention span. It is the best age for the encouragement of memorization of Scripture, for things now learned stick in the boy's mind often-times throughout his life. It is very difficult, on the other hand, for boys between eight and twelve to concentrate for any length of time. The best method for teaching, by far, is the story method, for due to his keen imagination and tendency to dramatize, the boy lives in a story and follows it through. It is not at all uncommon for a ten-year-old boy, having heard a vividly-told story just once, to be able to repeat it in its entirety a week or more later. To try to use other means of teaching besides stories or perhaps pictures, presents difficulties, because the boy's mind will wander and fail to follow the sequence of any sort of straight talk or sermonette.

5. The 8 to 12 age is the time of the most ready acceptance of authority. Normally boys of this period will not question the authority of adults, but will assume that obedience is to be taken for granted. Generally speaking, recurring disobedience among this age boys is the fault of the adult, for any failure of implicit obedience should be corrected quickly, pleasantly, and firmly. Confining limits and boundaries in games and activities are accepted largely without question. The boy has not yet come to the age of extreme curiosity that seemingly compels him to go beyond the limits to see what is beyond or simply to see what will happen.

6. The pre-adolescent period is the great time of formation of habits. During the previous period of infancy and earliest childhood, the governing force had been instinct. Now, during this period, habit largely controls, and health, reading, studying, and similar factors can be effectively channeled for the boy's future benefit.

7. This period of early boyhood is the time when hero worship is strongest. Unconsciously and even consciously a boy copies his father, his leader, and others whom worthy or not, he has chosen as his heroes. Significant in this connection is the fact that at this age much of the Old Testament is readily taught, particularly the stories of the great heroes of the Bible.

EARLY ADOLESCENCE 12 - 15   (PIONEER TRAILS AGE)

Adolescence is defined as both the process and the period of growing from childhood to maturity. The factor that leads from childhood to early adolescence is the time of puberty when the sexual organs are matured. In boys this is normally between twelve and fourteen. There is considerable variation in the exact time at which different fellows reach puberty and in the speed with which they develop. Such factors as sections of the country and climate, racial stock, and variation in early responsibility directly effect the speed with which a boy matures. Some fellows seem to sail through these maturing years on the crest of the wave, but most of them have times of discouragement when they especially crave understanding and when they are particularly susceptible to spiritual doubts and disturbances.

Five basic principles help to understand this period.

1. During the period of early adolescence comes a boy's most rapid and oftentimes most uneven growth. It is the uneveness of this maturing that often causes a fellow much distress — sort of psychological "growing pains." Jim, for instance, was six-foot-one when he was fifteen and seemed to be still growing. He was a well-built goodlooking fellow who ought to have taken real advantage of his height. But he didn't. He was always self-conscious about the fact that he was taller than any of his friends and was seriously worried for fear he wouldn't stop growing. He wouldn't stand up straight, but sort of stooped in order to conceal his height. Of course that made him more noticeable. The reason for his confusion was that while he had the physical bulk of a grown man, he was nevertheless a boy. In his social maturity he was retarded — about like the average thirteen-year-old. In a year or two, however, he reached a balance point and came out of it in good shape.

An alert leader will be careful not to embarrass the fellow going through this growing stage. By his understanding attitude, he will have opportunity to help the boy get through this period with a minimum of difficulty.

2. Entering adolescence is accompanied normally by definite development in social consciousness. During the time of infancy the boy's thoughts and actions were all centered in himself. In pre-adolescent boyhood he became aware of others and began to fit in his activities with others. He came to much prefer the company of other fellows to doing things by himself. Now, entering adolescence, altruistic tendencies assert themselves in terms of genuine interest in others. "Gang loyalty" is at its strongest, and true teamwork becomes possible. These fellows enjoy the highly organized athletic team games.

3. With adolescence, fellows begin to take interest in girls. At first they are apt to be awkward and ill at ease in their presence, but this is overcome with increasing maturity. Although interest in girls is now increasing, fellows as a rule still prefer to do things with other fellows, and their best friends are other boys.

4. The early adolescent boy's mind is developing. He is beginning to learn to think abstractly. At about fifteen the brain stops growing in size, and there are marked changes in a fellow's mental development. The popularity of slang might be attributed in part to the fact that in the very process of learning to think a fellow is discovering so many new thoughts that his vocabulary of accepted English is totally inadequate to express them.

5. As pre-adolescence was the period of authority when fellows accepted the direction and word of adults without much question, so contrariwise, now in adolescent years fellows tend to become independent and want to search out things for themselves.

The special danger in fellows thinking through great spiritual truths for themselves is that they may easily fall into a rut of false teaching. Probably the greatest number of false doctrines and heresies have arisen because individuals with immature and questioning minds took short cuts in their own thinking to fairly plausible explanations of things hard to understand, and used isolated Scriptures to back them

up. A fellow's doubts should be faced squarely, but solved by a careful
study of the Word.

MIDDLE ADOLESCENCE 15 - 18 (ADVANCED TRAILS AGE)

In the years fifteen to eighteen, many of the problems that have
been facing a fellow are clearing up. Fellows in this age group are
outstanding for leadership in Brigade. Some, however, are not leaders,
and the important difference between the leader. and the mere follower
in the group is seen in the relative ability to take responsibility.

Reaching his later teens, a boy ought to have some ideas in his mind
concerning his life work, and he should be making rather definite plans
in regard to preparation for that work or general field.

Three general characteristics can be laid down concerning fellows
in the middle adolescent period.

1. The middle adolescent age is the time when a boy approaches
his full physical growth and begins to fill out. He begins to overcome
adolescent awkwardness. Physical changes, rising out of development
of his sexual organs near completion at this time and his physical
maturity is progressing. It is a time for rigorous crafts and plenty of
competitive play.

2. "Advanced Trails" is a time of marked social development.
The boy emerges further from the "uncivilized" stage and begins to
accept the foibles of society and is in turn accepted by society. The
natural rebelliousness of the earlier changing years against rules begins
to balance out into a more understanding attitude.. The boy's interest
in girls develops further and he begins to "go steady." Many fellows,
especially in certain strata of society, marry during this time and prove
sufficiently mature to make good homes and take the responsibilities of
full maturity. The trend of improved education, however, is to delay
the time of marriage, thus allowing more time for the preparation
job which boyhood is called upon to do.

Leadership training is especially valuable during this time.

3. In the 15 to 18 age group a boy begins to do things from a more
mature point of view and begins to exercise mental initiative. There is
the urge to create, and the boy is more capable of following through in
taking responsibilities for doing things on his own. The lives of most

great men have consisted of their carrying through in later years the ideals formulated in this period.

The doubts and questions of early adolescence are now being settled in one way or another, and the boy establishes somewhat of a philosophy of life. He has more appreciation for the adult's viewpoint and is much more willing to accept authority, because he has now learned through his own thinking the wisdom of following the advice of those more mature.

The program for this age boy must be geared to a high plane of achievement and there must be ample room for creative and futuristic thinking.

*   *   *   *   *   *   *

This chapter on boys has not been an attempt to put every boy into a definite pattern of characteristics. To do that would require a good deal more space than this manual has available! The leader will undoubtedly be coming into contact with boys who do not in some way fit the characteristics that have been listed. However, in the main, the material does apply to boys everywhere, for it consists of basic, general facts. It furnishes, then, a valuable working foundation in boys' work for each leader to adapt to the local situation.

CHAPTER OUTLINE

ACHIEVEMENT CHALLENGE

ACHIEVEMENT PROGRESS

CHAPTER TWO

A Boy's Program – Brigade Achievement

ACHIEVEMENT CHALLENGE

When a fellow first comes into contact with Christian Service Brigade and first looks over his BOY'S GUIDEBOOK or STOCKADER'S LOG, he finds open before him an exciting adventure trail — the path of Brigade Achievement. It is the answer to all three of the boy's basic urges, for it enables him to *be*, to *do*, and to *learn*.

What lies beyond the tallest trees — beyond the vast, silent forest — beyond the furthest ridge of mountains? To find the answer, one must climb the ridge, and with climbing comes growth, a reaching of higher levels, achievement.

The urge to explore and pioneer is a part of every boy. He wants to see beyond the ridge. The Brigade program is built on that principle, for it enables a boy to climb — to accept the challenge of achievement! And as he climbs in the Achievement program he will be growing into full Christian manhood.

The program itself appeals to the boy both because it leads to heights of accomplishment — the distant snow-capped peaks — and because immediately before him there is activity-achievement well within his reach — the near foothills, themselves holding hidden territory to be explored.

Because it is true that every boy wants to be top-notch, one of the greatest means of guiding his achievement is the setting up of standards. When a man who has gained the confidence of boys says, either by actual statement of standards or by example and illustration, "*This* is what it is to be a first-rater," those boys will do their best to live up to that standard.

The terminology and theme behind the presentation of the Brigade Achievement program follow the thought of the pioneering and exploration of natural frontiers. It appeals, thus, to the pioneering spirit that is so large a part of our heritage and history. Also, the pioneering theme is fittingly analogous to the program of Christ for reaching out to the spiritual frontiers of the world with the message of the Gospel.

Early in the history of climbing someone must have discovered that the process is greatly facilitated by steps. Brigade's Achievement program advances according to steps, each one of which, when accomplished, brings a boy within reach of another, higher stage of advancement.

Building a natural sequence in a boy's progress, each step is a recognized victory in itself, yet also part of his total achievement and a fair measure of his full-rounded Christian growth.

The boy of eight, beginning Brigade, enters the Stockade. Here, though still within sheltering walls, he none-the-less begins his preparation for the pioneering ahead. Inside the Stockade there is opportunity to achieve as he proves himself in Stockader activities and becomes in order a STOCKADE BUILDER (earning four or more *Blockhouses*), then a STOCKADE SENTINEL (earning four or more *Stations*).

The twelve-year-old boy, whether coming out of Stockade or starting out new in the Brigade Battalion, works first on his Pioneer Trails. These are sometimes referred to as the "Basic Three," for they are the center of the Brigade Achievement program. The first rank, EXPLORER, is looking for a trail — he is searching out the truth, especially the truth of God as revealed in Christ. He learns the landmarks by which the trail is recognized.

When he has found the trail, the Explorer goes on to become a TRAILBLAZER, to mark the trail well so that others may follow it. He leads a trailmate along the path and shows him the old landmarks which he has found.

The final step in the Pioneer Trails is reached when the Trailblazer becomes a GUIDE. Now he not only knows the trail and is able to help others along, but he has gone over the whole trail carefully and is ready to guide others on it.

The Guide stands at the top of the ridge looking on to hills and valleys and still higher mountains ahead. Now there is a vast amount of territory before him for exploration, and he can choose in which direction he will go. Four different main paths in the Advanced Trails are before him: AIRMAN, MARINER, WOODSMAN, and RANGER. Each of the first three specializes in a certain field. The fourth, Ranger, roams the fields of different crafts and has a large elective choice. All these ranks cover the same territory in the study of the Word, namely, certain great doctrines of the Bible and the reading of twelve of the books of the Old Testament.

When he has chosen his field, the Guide, who must be over fourteen before beginning the Advanced Trails, may earn three advancements within the specialized trail. For each of these he is awarded a star. A three-star Airman, Mariner, Woodsman, or Ranger is eligible to work for the peak of Brigade earned achievement, the HERALD OF CHRIST.

The Herald emerges from the Brigade Achievement program with a much different life outlook than the Stockader who entered some years back — coming in then a little boy with little-boy ideas about big things, he grew through the formative years, molded his ideals and ambitions, made life decisions and probably chose the field of his life work.

As a Herald, he stands now a man, ready to do the work of a man for his Lord.

ACHIEVEMENT PROGRESS

As a boy goes forward in his achievement in Brigade, each step is a mark of spiritual growth. For as a guide to boy action, the program leads a boy through a full round of activities which are of vital interest to him, helps him to achieve in each one, and guides him in correlating each one with his spiritual life as a Christian.

A great deal of emphasis is put on the reading, study, and memorization of the Scriptures, not as incidental, but as integral to a full life. This principle of correlation between Christian teaching and everyday living is of tremendous significance in the Christian education of boys.

In the process of advancing through the entire Achievement program (taking from the time he enters Stockade at the age of eight until he receives the rank of Brigade Herald, no less than eight and probably ten years later) a boy has made deeply significant progress.

He has read through the entire Bible, reading certain sections, if not all, on a chapter-a-day basis and with careful study. The reading order of the books is calculated to have followed best his spiritual and mental maturing.

He has memorized for use well over 100 key Scripture verses.

He has grown in leadership from the bringing of three visitors to a Stockade meeting to the place where he has planned and led Squad and Battalion meetings and helped in planning camping and other specialized activities.

He has followed in the years of his progress an organized health program with periodical, thorough self-checkup.

He has entered into a study of Christian missions through the reading of missionary books and the study of the lives of great pioneer missionaries.

He has taken active part in a wide variety of activities — team athletics, swimming, hiking, explorations, camping, and project construction. And the sequence of these is arranged to have developed his keeness of insight and perception, his skill, his coordination, and especially his resourcefulness.

He has earned at least 29 Brigade craft certificates, each one qualifying him as familiar with a certain field of activity. And he has also thought about and explained how activity in each of those varied fields can contribute to his witness for the Lord Jesus Christ.

In the Brigade Pledge: "Trusting in the Lord Jesus Christ, and in Him alone as my Savior, I as a Brigadier purpose in my heart to live Bright and Keen for Christ that I may glorify Him," (also in the Seven Points of Valor: Honor, Courage, Chivalry, Purity, Loyalty, Obedience, and Consecration) the thoughts of the achieving boy are directly channeled to think seriously about the question of his own relationship to the Lord Jesus both in regard to salvation and in regard to Christian living.

Each time a boy passes an Achievement test he is brought into personal, private contact with a commissioned officer who is qualified as a consecrated Christian man to be a spiritual leader of boys. And a good opportunity is afforded for that man in a natural way to talk to the boy about the Lord.

*   *   *   *   *   *   *

The Brigade Achievement program is a key factor in Brigade. It meets all three of the boy's basic urges — to be, to do, and to learn. It is the cohesive agent in the over-all program, and most important of all, it is the instrument through which the leader can most readily accomplish the Brigade aim of winning and training boys. The leader who personally understands and then intelligently uses the Achievement program has made one of his biggest steps in progress toward effective work with boys.

CHAPTER OUTLINE

THE BATTALION; SQUADS

THE BATTALION ORGANIZATION

Battalion Sponsorship
Battalion Leadership
Battalion Membership

THE BATTALION AND THE CHURCH

It will bring the boys to the church
It will vitalize the boys' relationship to the church
It will hold the boys in the church
It will train the boys for leadership
It will provide a bond of fellowship between the boys and the men of the church
It will provide for the men of the church challenge and opportunity for service
It will strengthen the position of the church in the community

THE BATTALION AND CHRISTIAN SERVICE BRIGADE

THE STOCKADE

Stockade Theme
Stockade Organization

CHAPTER THREE

A Boy's Club – Brigade Battalion

THE BATTALION; SQUADS

A whirl of action with a gang of keen fellows laughing, working, playing, and learning under wide-awake men and boy leaders — that's the picture of a Brigade BATTALION, the Christ-centered boys' club. The word "Battalion" itself is used in the basic sense of a group organized for action.

The Battalion is the channel through which the Achievement program is actually presented to boys. It forms the common meeting ground for boys, leaders, and program.

With relation to sponsorship, the Battalion is an integral part of the local church program, for Christian Service Brigade is not something extra added as a special system of activities to augment the church program. Brigade *is* the church, reaching into the real and rightful sphere of interest in boys everywhere.

To the point of view of the individual boy coming into Brigade, his Battalion is his "gang." It is a "gang" that does a number of very specific things for him. (1) It gives him fellowship with a group of boys his own age, generally with like interests to his own, who are predominantly Christian fellows; very significantly the leaders among the fellows in the group — those to whom he looks with respect — are the most spiritual among the gang. (2) It gives him the realization that he has a place in the organized part of the church program. (3) It gives him regular and profitable contact with spiritual leaders of the church who are in charge of the Battalion. (4) It presents to him an appealing activity program into which to direct his increasing energies. (5) It guides his thinking, from week to week and during the week, through Battalion activities, toward spiritual growth.

Within the Battalion are SQUADS. These are groups of from four to eight fellows who work together as a unit.

Squads are of prime importance in answering discipline problems, providing juinor leadership training, and promoting Battalion growth. As a unit in a Battalion, the Squad takes special advantage of the natural gang spirit.

THE BATTALION ORGANIZATION

To understand the organization of the Brigade Battalion itself, three factors must be considered: SPONSORSHIP — the local church and its representative Battalion Committee; LEADERSHIP — the Captain and his Lieutenants and junior leaders; and MEMBERSHIP — the boys themselves.

Battalion Sponsorship

The BATTALION is the church's own boys' club, fully constituted as an integral part of the church's program of evangelism and training. Hence, the initiative for its establishment comes from within the local church. Men of the church — pastors, officials, fathers — burdened for the salvation of boys and seeing the need of an outreach of the church's program directly for boys, consider and pray. Contacting headquarters of Christian Service Brigade, they receive necessary information, and the church takes official action in forming a BATTALION COMMITTEE.

The Battalion Committee consists of three or more men of the church. chosen to be responsible for the Battalion. The Committee is authorized to represent the church in planning and establishing the Battalion and to choose the man to become the Battalion CAPTAIN.

The individual leader of the Battalion who is in regular contact with the boys themselves, the Brigade Captain, must first be elected by the Battalion Committee and then receive a commission to the rank of Captain from Brigade Headquarters.

Christian men of the church and community who are vitally interested in boys, and therefore in the work of the Battalion, may become Senior members of Brigade as BRIGADE DADS.

The more men there are in the church or community who feel themselves a part of the Brigade program, the better the situation for the local Battalion. For then the Captain and his assistants, the Committee, and the boys can count on the active interest of those men in their work. As Brigade Dads these men share in praying for the work, share financially in the Brigade program, carry a Brigade membership card similiar to the one carried by the boys themselves, and wear the Brigade pin.

Battalion Leadership

The Captain is the man in command of the Battalion and as such responsible to the Committee. His job is primarily one of spiritual leadership and of program integration.

The Lieutenant (there may be several) is the Captain's assistant, a man fellowshipping right with him in the work. Except for the special work of integrating the whole program, the Lieutenant's work is exactly the same as the Captain's. He is commissioned from Headquarters in the same manner as the Captain and is active as counsellor of boys.

If the pastor or any of the committeemen is able to be present regularly and takes active part in the Battalion meeting, he should be commissioned as a Lieutenant to make clear his position of helping the Captain.

Non-commissioned officers in the Battalion (Sergeants, Corporals, and Lance-Corporals) are boys chosen from the ranks and appointed by the Captain. Their rating as non-commissioned officers is quite separate from their earned Achievement ranks such as Explorer or Trailblazer, but their progress in Achievement is always taken into consideration when they are appointed.

The Sergeant is responsible for the smooth running of the Battalion meeting, for all formations, and for the keeping of order generally.

Each Corporal is responsible for the leadership of a Squad and for the conduct of its members during Squad meetings and formations. He is also responsible for the stimulation of his fellows in their Achievement progress. Some of the best teaching a Captain can do is through his Corporals. Lance-corporals are second-in-command in their Squads and are in training for corporalcy, ready to take over the leadership of the Squad in the absence of the corporal.

Battalion Membership

The Brigade Battalion is the local church's own boys' club. Yet, in relation to the community as a whole and especially with regard to boys, it is open for all boys, regardless of church connection or lack of church connection. Boys are welcome to participate in Battalion activities without discrimination as to background.

The only limit which is placed on boy participation in the Battalion is a minimum age boundary. Boys must be twelve years old or older to become Battalion members. Younger boys between the ages of eight and eleven are provided for in the Stockade program. There is no upper age limit for Battalion participation, but the local group should reach boys up to the age of eighteen. It is in order that these older fellows might be reached and the program remain of vital interest to them that the lower age limit has been set.

Boys may become Battalion members when they have attended three Battalion meetings. Their names are then sent to Brigade Headquarters together with the twenty-five cent registration fee, and they receive their official membership cards. Their membership is renewed each year through the annual Battalion registration.

It is recommended that the maximum size of a Battalion not exceed four Squads of eight boys each, plus the necessary leadership. When the Battalion is reaching more than this maximum, it is wise to begin another Battalion. This size standard applies also to the Stockade.

THE BATTALION AND THE CHURCH

(Seven Things a *Strong* Battalion Will Do For Your Church)

All of these seven points are not only things that a strong Battalion *can* do for the church. They are what the normal Battalion *should* be doing for the church. They are listed, then, in this chapter to give the leader an idea of what to expect from his own Brigade group in relation to the sponsoring church.

It will bring the boys to the church.

The Brigade Battalion is actually the church reaching out to the boys of the community with a vital, appealing boy-program. Drawing them to Brigade, the activity is thereby drawing them also to the church. Basically and throughout its program, Brigade is a means of evangelism. The Gospel witness is continually extended to the boys, and through the boys to their chums. As unsaved boys are won for Christ and begin to grow in Him, they grow also in their desire for the spiritual fellowship and nourishment of the church.

A secondary factor is the reaching of the parents. New families in the community, as well as the unchurched, usually gravitate to the church of their children's choice. Thus the appeal to boys frequently results also in reaching new families for the church.

It will vitalize the boys' relationship to the church.

Through the Battalion, the church is interpreted on a boy level. Recognizing it is an integral part of the total church program, the boy sees that his service in the Battalion is service in the church — and service which a boy and only a boy can do. Now in a new way he can take pride in his church and feel that he is a part of it. Through his activity with the Battalion, the boy receives a vision of service to the Lord Jesus in the local church which is basic to effective Christian living throughout his life.

It will hold boys in the church.

Because the church is made real to boys through their Battalion, they have a real basis for loyalty to the church. The average church loses seventy per cent of its boys when they reach adolescent years. Out of one hundred boys in the primary department of the average Sunday School only twenty are held through the senior department. Yet the church must depend in coming years on this depleted boy group for the bulk of its male leadership. The value of Brigade here is obvious, for the Battalion program is filled with activities for the very fellows who normally begin to lose interest and drop out of the church.

The Battalion will hold these fellows in the church, first, because the activities of the Battalion are of vital interest to them; second, because the church has become real to them and they feel a part of it; last and most important of all, because as they advance in Brigade Achievement and in understanding of the Word and of spiritual things, they will also grow in hunger for the Word and for Christian fellowship. And in the final analysis, there is no better nor surer motive for loyalty to the church than a real heart hunger for the things of Christ found in the church.

It will train boys for leadership.

The Brigade Achievement program is also fundamentally a training program, and its correlation with the skills and activities of everyday living make it a training program for Christian leadership in every phase of life. The Battalion will provide the church a primary means for its part in beginning the preparation of Christian leaders for the business and industrial world, for government, for the professions. It is further an invaluable training ground for boys planning missionary service and other full-time Christian work.

Of more direct consequence to the individual church, the spiritual training of the Battalion program will provide greatly needed consecrated Christian leadership for the church of future years. Acceptance of their leadership responsibility in the church will come natural when fellows have been given opportunity as boys to fill positions of leadership in the church Battalion.

It will provide a bond of fellowship between the boys and the men of the church.

Often in churches today the men find their own spheres of interests and the boys find theirs, and there is little opportunity for the boys to profit by the fellowship and example of Christian men. In the modern home, too, the average father finds much too little opportunity for personal contact with his own sons.

Thus the Battalion fills a real need in providing occasion for spiritual fellowship between fathers and sons, men and boys.

The Brigade Dad program provides for the local Battalion to be augmented by a "Dads Club" consisting of men of the church willing to do a 'dad's job" for boys in winning them for Christ and in helping them to grow in Him. Some of these Dads may be actively engaged in the leadership of the Battalion as Captain or Lieutenants, others stand behind the work as Committeemen; still others are craft guides ready to counsel boys who want to learn something of their field of specialization. Then there are those who have none of these functional responsibilities but stand behind the work with their prayers and interest and are ready to be pals to boys in general. All of these men are a part of Brigade, partners with the boys.

It will provide for the men of the church challenge and opportunity for service.

The Battalion in the church is an outlet for service that depends entirely upon the church's men for leadership. Here is ample opportunity for pastor and layman to unite in accomplishing a vital part of the church's program.

Men will serve as actual Battalion leaders, as Committeemen for the local group, and as Brigade Dads in backing up the work. For the leaders, provision is made for the training of the layman for effective leadership among boys, with helps and materials supplied to aid in his work. All of the men in the Brigade program have a common bond of fellowship and a realization of accomplishment in serving the church.

It will strengthen the position of the church in the community.

The church is judged by the people of the community according to its ability to cope with the problems which confront the community, and by the way it fulfills what they conceive to be its local responsibility. One problem which is a matter of vital concern to nearly every community, and whose solution should be considered by every church as its solemn responsibility, is the much discussed problem of youth delinquency.

In the local community this problem is not interpreted in terms of mass statistics and trends, but rather in terms of the local boy that got into trouble or the truant from school who is on his way in that direction. The community asks the church, "What can you do about him?"

Although the church of Jesus Christ has the only completely adequate answer to the juvenile crime problem, yet unless the church's program

includes an effective channel whereby it can reach the boys in need —
usually the hardest to reach — it is not equipped to fulfill its responsibility to the community. The Battalion can reach those boys, bring them
into the company of top-notch Christian fellows, guide them into
worthy expenditure of their energies, and most of all, present to them a
Saviour who is real to a regular fellow and can meet his needs.

Even aside from the question of what the church can do about boy
delinquency, the Battalion can have a great deal of effect on the church's
acceptance in the eyes of the community. One of the chief functions of
the Brigade program, in relation to the individual boy, is the correlation
of the Christian teaching of the church with the fellow's daily life and
contacts. When boys in their contacts with neighbors and associates
demonstrate in practical everyday living the fact that they are Christians,
then the church is known by its fruit. Through athletic events and
various other phases of the Battalion's through-the-year program, there
is plenty of opportunity for the people of the community to see the
Brigade fellows in action. All of these things witness to the effectiveness of the total program of the local church.

THE BATTALION AND CHRISTIAN SERVICE BRIGADE

Christian Service Brigade is a national organization and each local
Brigade Battalion has a definite relationship in this organization. The
main factors in this relationship are: local authority, Board of Directors,
Brigade Staff Officer, Brigade Headquarters, Area Organization, and
Division Organization.

First, as to LOCAL AUTHORITY, the Battalion is under the direct authority and responsibility of its Battalion Committee. One part of the
Committee's responsibility is to see that the Battalion meets and maintains
the standards set by Christian Service Brigade for active Battalions. The
standards have been set both to keep the individual Battalion at maximum
effectiveness in using the Brigade program, and also to maintain the
standing of Brigade as a national organization.

Christian Service Brigade has been chartered as an organization
for the "non-sectarian Christian education of youth." To carry out this
purpose it is organized as a mission board to work with local churches

to win and train boys for Christ, and it is under the direction of a BOARD OF DIRECTORS. This Board, composed of men from all walks of life serving as members on a voluntary basis, oversees the work and sets the policies by which the work is run. As related to the local Battalion, the existence of the Board safeguards and guides the testimony, program, and use of men and money in this work of which the Battalion is a part.

The STAFF OFFICERS of Brigade are called into the work on a missionary basis by the Board of Directors. One of the concerns of these men is to help the individual Battalions and leaders as much as possible. They do not themselves run local Battalions, but through leadership training courses, analysis of problems, and personal suggestions seek to strengthen each Battalion. In some cases staff men are responsible for a specific territory, while in other cases they have specialized duties such as publications or the general secretaryship.

BRIGADE HEADQUARTERS in Chicago is the coordinating center of the Brigade work. It supplies Brigade materials to the Battalions, keeps Headquarters records of all Battalions, handles the leader training course, gives information to and follows through on churches interested in establishing Battalions, and in general is the clearing house for Brigade contact wherever that contact may be.

Like the Battalion, the BRIGADE AREA has full local authority in its particular sphere of activity. And it, too, is organized and maintained on established standards. Although given Headquarters' assistance where necessary, the Area is begun and carried on entirely by the constituent Battalions.

The BRIGADE DIVISION is a sectional grouping of areas and Battalions to allow for the most efficient work of the Staff Officer. These Divisions are not permanent, but may vary with the progress and circumstances of the work.

THE STOCKADE

The Stockade is the Brigade program for the 8-11 age boy. It is entirely separate from the Battalion program. The Achievement work and weekly meeting are carefully designed for this age boy; he has his own manual, the STOCKADER'S LOG, and other distinctive equipment. As a Stockader he carries the Stockade membership card.

The Stockade unit is an important part of the church's boys work program. As in the case of the Battalion, it is more than a mere recreation outlet — it is a key means of winning and training the junior age boy for Christ.

Stockade Theme

The theme of the Stockade terminology, carried throughout both its Achievement ranks and its leadership positions, follows the lore surrounding the log stockades built by early American settlers. Blockhouses, Builders, Sentinels, Lookouts, Couriers, and similar terms each have their counterpart in pioneering history.

Within the walls of the stockade were kept those who were young and not yet prepared to brave the trails of the forest. To them the stockade was a place for preparation. Likewise, the Brigade Stockade is a place of preparation for further adventure in the Battalion activities of exploring Pioneer Trails.

Stockade Organization

To be fully effective, each Stockade unit needs a Battalion into which to send the boys at 12 years of age. Here the early adolescent boy will find the challenge of Pioneer Trails activities. Likewise, the Battalion is greatly strengthened by a strong Stockade program which prepares the pre-adolescent boy in a full round of Achievement and activitiy. Together, these two units form a coordinated boys work for the local church.

As indicated in the organizing materials, the most effective method of organizing these units is to give the Battalion precedence. That is, where both groups cannot be organized at the same time or with equal emphasis, the Battalion should be organized first. When the Battalion is well established, the Stockade can then be organized for the younger boys. Experience has amply demonstrated the wisdom of this, for it is only natural for younger fellows to follow older fellows.

THE STOCKADE COMMITTEE

One committee, the Boys' Work Committee of the church, is responsible for both the Battalion and Stockade. Often certain committee members represent especially the Stockade or the Battalion. With regard to the Stockade, the committee has the same duties as outlined elsewhere for Battalion committee work.

THE STOCKADE RANGER

In the Stockade the commissioned adult leader is called a Ranger. The equivalent to the Battalion Captain is the Chief Ranger. The full Stockade will be led by one Chief Ranger and four or more Rangers. (Note: the title "Ranger" is given only when earned by completing the leader training requirement; otherwise, adult helpers are called "Guides.")

Leadership qualifications given in this manual (Chapter Four) and other leadership suggestions (e.g., Chapter Seven) apply equally to Stockade and Battalion leaders. All men participating in the Stockade work, regardless of position, should become as familiar as possible with the STOCKADER'S LOG and the contents of this manual.

CHAPTER OUTLINE

FIVE BASIC "MUSTS" FOR A CHRISTIAN LEADER
OF BOYS

1. *A keen love for boys.*
2. *A sound appreciation of the job to be done.*
3. *A firm foundation in the Word of God.*
4. *A sincere application of every talent to the job.*
5. *A consistent testimony in daily Christian living.*

SPECIFIC BRIGADE STANDARDS FOR BATTALION
CAPTAINCY

1. *He must be a born-again Christian.*
2. *He must be a man.*
3. *He must be 21 years of age or older.*
4. *He must subscribe to the standard of faith.*
5. *He must declare his leadership purpose.*
6. *He must maintain a Christian tstimony.*
7. *He must be willing to prepare for leadership.*

CHAPTER FOUR

A Boy's Leader - Brigade Captain

The fourth factor in Brigade is the boys' leader, the Brigade Captain. He is the vital spark in the program — the man whose personal contact with the boys is the moving force in winning and training them for Christ. This manual has been prepared for his use, to enable him to do his work effectively.

The leader's responsibility is large. He is to be a living example and personal counsellor for his boys, and is to take a definite position of leadership in the church and community. He is also the representative of Christian Service Brigade as a national organization to the church, community, and boys. For these reasons it is of great importance that he be fully qualified for the work before undertaking the job of being a Brigade Captain.

FIVE BASIC "MUSTS" FOR A CHRISTIAN LEADER OF BOYS.

1. A keen love for boys
2. A sound appreciation of the job to be done
3. A firm foundation in the Word of God
4. A sincere application of every talent to the job
5. A consistent testimony in daily Christian living

These five basic factors equip a man for his great work of being a leader of boys. Lacking any one of them, a man cannot effectively serve God among boys. To demonstrate further their importance, each point is now considered individually.

A keen love for boys

To do one's best in anything requires genuine interest. So with the Captain. There must be that warmth of feeling in his work that comes

41

from loving those fellows entrusted to his guidance. With that
love will come a care for their souls and heart interest in fellows who
are not Christians — a fervent desire to see them come to know Christ.
Genuine love for the boys will keep the Captain going when things get
tough and obstacles arise, and he'll need love for the difficult fellows
and the problem fellows. In bringing your work before the Lord,
Captain, ask always for a large measure of love for your boys, for it's
a first essential.

A sound appreciation of the job to be done

A Captaincy, if worth taking, is worth taking seriously. Upon
accepting his commission, the Captain becomes a leader of boys. There
is a responsibility beyond the leading of meetings or planning of programs.
His is the responsibility of boys — boys with souls and lives. That means
a realization of the importance of his position and a conscientous application to details, from getting to meetings on time to dealing with
his boys about salvation. Church, community, parents, and above all,
boys are looking to him.

A firm foundation in the Word of God

In himself, each of us is basically inadequate for the spiritual
requirements of dealing with boys. But we have the Word of God which
does the work. Understanding the Bible in order to make it real to the
boys is one of the Captain's prime responsibilities. It is especially necessary for the leader of boys to be a student of the Bible, for to minister
to the spiritual needs of boys requires (perhaps more than in any other
group) readiness for "on the spur of the moment" answers.

Often this "out of season" kind of teaching — being able to supply
from the Word the answer to the question at hand — will make the
deepest impression. Study of the Bible will lead to fruitful leadership,
as well as personal profit and enjoyment.

A sincere application of every talent to the job

An abundance of talents is not essential to good leadership. The
consecration of talent to full use is essential. No man can be an expert

in all the activities, hobbies, and crafts that come into the Brigade program. Yet many men have their own hobbies or have developed a skill along certain lines that can be of real help in the work, for every boy admires a leader who "knows his stuff."

One essential talent is the ability to analyse boys, program, and problems in order to deal effectively with each. The Captain will do well to consider and develop this ability.

Athletic leadership is a valuable asset to the Captain who is capable of it. It is often the key to a fellow who seems otherwise unreachable. Stamina to keep up with his boys, energy and vitality to spark Battalion activities, and general sparkle of life go a long way toward successful leadership. Enthusiastic and vigorous leadership can put across the most difficult or disagreeable task. The Captain who cannot exercise athletic leadership himself should have a Lieutenant who takes that part of the program. Each Battalion should have at least one leader to spark sports, hikes, woodsmanship, and the like.

A consistent testimony in daily Christian living

The Captain in Brigade is more than a director of the weekly boys' club program. He is an example of Christian living for the boys in that club.

What he says and does in presenting the Brigade program and in meeting with his fellows is all prefaced by what his life says and does.

The following paragraphs are given to aid the Captain in considering the standards of his own Christian life in relation to his work with boys.

THE LEADER'S LIFE SHOULD BE POSITIVE. A hesitant, uncertain Christian testimony will greatly undermine the effectiveness of the Gospel appeal to the boys. The Christian leader should be certain of his own relation to Christ and happy in it.

THE LEADER'S LIFE SHOULD BE WITHOUT QUESTION. His personal habits must be such that the boys who listen to him at the Brigade meeting on Thursday, can observe him on Friday without losing respect for his testimony. What that will mean with regard to the common "questionable practices" of theater attendance, use of tobacco, use of liquor, dancing, card playing, and indecent language will be obvious.

From the viewpoint of Christian Service Brigade these practices are not consistent 'with the unquestionable testimony required of one who seeks to be a Christian leader of boys. For that man has the overwhelmingly serious job of shaping lives. He cannot be too careful.

There are also other phases of living a clear-cut testimony which are sometimes not as obvious as the "questionable practices." Temper, dishonesty, pride, — such as these may well be question marks that need to be subjected before the leader's testimony carries weight.

To some leaders these standards of Christian living may be a real problem. They should be a challenge to all. The Lord's service requires clean vessels, and He has promised the grace necessary to be such. Brigade does not expect "perfect" leaders. It does trust the Lord will give men who can stand before boys with a positive, clear-cut Christian life, and in turn have the joy of watching boys follow them into a similar life.

SPECIFIC BRIGADE STANDARDS FOR BATTALION CAPTAINCY.

The Battalion Captain is chosen by the Battalion Committee. Before he can be officially recognized as the leader of the Battalion, however, he must be commissioned to the rank of Captain directly from Brigade Headquarters. This commission is granted on the condition that all of the following seven specific requirements are met:

1. He must be a born-again Christian. This is, of course, the basic requirement for one who is entering into Christian service.

2. He must be a man. The whole Brigade set-up is distinctly a masculine affair, and requires a man as leader to be effective.

3. He must be 21 years of age or older. The responsibilities that fall upon a Captain require a mature man for the job.

4. He must subscribe to the following standard of faith prior to his recognition or commission by Brigade Headquarters:

STANDARD OF FAITH OF CHRISTIAN SERVICE BRIGADE

a. We believe in the Scriptures of the Old and the New Testaments as verbally inspired by God and inerrant in the original writing, and that they are of supreme and final authority in faith and life.

b. We believe in one God, eternally existing in three Persons: Father, Son, and Holy Spirit.

c. We believe that Jesus Christ was begotten by the Holy Spirit, born of the Virgin Mary, and is true God and true man.

d. We believe that man was created in the image of God; that he sinned and thereby incurred, not only physical death, but also that spiritual death which is separation from God; and that all human beings are born with a sinful nature, and, in the case of those who reach moral responsibility, become sinners in thought, word, and deed.

e. We believe that the Lord Jesus died for our sins, according to the Scriptures, as a representative and substituitionary sacrifice; and that all who believe in Him are justified on the ground of His shed blood.

f. We believe in the resurrection of the crucified body of our Lord, in His ascension into Heaven, and in His present life there for us, as High Priest and Advocate.

g. We believe in the personal and imminent return of our Lord and Saviour, Jesus Christ.

h. We believe that all who receive by faith the Lord Jesus Christ are born again of the Holy Spirit, and thereby become children of God.

i. We believe in the bodily resurrection of the just and the unjust, the everlasting blessedness of the saved, and the everlasting punishment of the lost.

5. He must declare his purpose in undertaking the work of leadership in Brigade among boys. The basic reason for entering the work must be for winning boys to the Lord Jesus Christ and for helping Christian fellows to grow in Him. Every man commissioned must have objectives beyond the purely social or secular.

6. He must declare his attitude toward Brigade's standards of Christian living as explained in this chapter and must live a consistent daily Christian life.

7. He must have become well acquainted with the Brigade program (through the study of the BOY'S GUIDEBOOK and STOCKADER'S LOG and this leader's manual) prior to his undertaking active leadership in the work. In connection with this manual a prepared course in leadership training will be used.

CHAPTER OUTLINE

STOCKADE ACHIEVEMENT

Stockade Builder
Stockade Sentinel
Achievement Records

PIONEER ACHIEVEMENT TRAILS

Brigade Explorer
Brigade Trailblazer
Brigade Guide

ADVANCED ACHIEVEMENT TRAILS

Brigade Ranger
Brigade Woodsman
Brigade Mariner
Brigade Airman

THE BRIGADE HERALD

CRAFTS IN THE BRIGADE PROGRAM

ACHIEVEMENT AWARD   CEREMONIES

CHAPTER FIVE

Achievement in Action

This is the first of the three "how" chapters. Its purpose is to give the leader a working knowledge of Brigade Achievement, that is, to equip him to actually use the Achievement program with boys.

In order to present Achievement as a connected unit, the program is presented right through from the Stockade on. In the newly established Battalion the Stockade Achievement cannot, of course, be taken into account until sometime later when it becomes feasible to establish also a Stockade.

If the leader has not yet read the STOCKADER'S LOG and BOY'S GUIDEBOOK, he should by all means do so before going into this discussion. Thorough acquaintanceship with the LOG and GUIDE-BOOK will both make this section easier to be understood and increase its value for future use.

STOCKADE ACHIEVEMENT

The sequence of activity through which the Stockade Achievement program leads a boy is geared to his own age level. At an age of rapid physical growth where the play instinct is strongest, he is given ample opportunity for physical activity. His mental processes are sharpening and he learns quickly, memorizes readily, and is in the habit-forming period. These tendencies are utilized in his progress as a Stockader. This is also the period of awakening consciousness of others. Thus, learning to live and work and play together with other fellows in Stockade is another valuable help for the boy.

Stockade Achievement has two age-level divisions. The first section is called the Stockade BUILDER and is for the 8 and 9 year old; the Stockade SENTINEL is the section for the 10 and 11 year old. The BUILDER and SENTINEL are ranks which the boy earns. However, each rank is composed of smaller Achievement units—called *Blockhouses* in the Builder rank; called *Stations* in the Sentinel rank.

In each rank there are four basic units *(Blockhouses* or *Stations).* The boy is given recognition for each unit completed as well as for achieving the full Builder or Sentinel rank. After receiving the rank pin (upon completion of the four basic units), he may then keep working to achieve more *Blockhouses* or *Stations* until he advances into the Sentinel Achievement step or enters the Battalion. These "extra" units are called *Outposts.*

After a boy has become a member of the Stockade (i.e., upon attending three regular meetings) he is eligible to receive either a Builder or Sentinel emblem, depending on his age. *Blockhouse* or *Station* awards are added to this emblem as they are earned. The emblem is worn on the Stockade jacket: Builder, right side; Sentinel, left side. These awards are illustrated on page 14 of the LOG.

Stockade Builder (LOG, pp. 15-80)

Each Builder *Blockhouse* (or Sentinel *Station*) follows a basic pattern, but has a variety as well. Each unit contains a story, Scripture memory work, Handyman project, and special activity. Often woven into this pattern are safety, emergency suggestions, Brigade lore, and other items. A brief analysis of the Builder rank will show how these all fit together.

1. *Stories.* Scripture based stories introduce each of the *Blockhouse* units. These stories are about Christ, David, Daniel, Joseph, etc. The stories are for the Stockader to read. In addition they can be read aloud by the Ranger, told in the Stockade meeting, or supplemented by Bible reading. To qualify for his Achievement record check, the boy should be able to review the main idea of the story. Encourage your Stockaders to read other Bible stories also.

2. *Memory Treasures.* The "treasure" of Scripture verses for the Stockader to learn take advantage of what has been called the "golden age of memorization." Every unit has a set of verses for memorization, and the verses have been chosen carefully for this age. This is an important opportunity to get God's Word into the hearts of the boys, and it is often

the means of dealing personally with a boy about his relationship with the Lord. Be sure to give special help to those who have trouble memorizing and to those to whom the Bible may be quite new. It is well to explain words or thoughts that may be difficult for this age boy to understand.

3. *Handyman Projects.* A wide variety of projects are suggested in the Handyman Storehouse (LOG, pp. 69-76) to allow for the different interests and abilities in the group. They can be worked on at the Stockade meeting (during Post time as a Sparker activity) and also done by the boy at home. The choosing of projects and the work on them usually requires the guidance of a leader.

The leader should plan on occasional demonstrations of the tools mentioned in the various Handyman sections. Some boys may not have access to the tools at home, and they should have the opportunity to become acquainted with them to meet the Achievement requirements. Outstanding Christian men in the church may assist you in this.

In giving credit for Handyman projects, the leader should encourage good work. Do not permit a boy to "get by" with a poor job when he could have done much better. On the other hand, it is not necessary to expect professional work. Judge the project on the basis of what the boy has done with the ability he has. When projects have been completed and checked, list them on the Handyman Record, p. 76.

4. *Action Projects.* Included in this section are practical home projects as well as many physical development items. As in the Handyman section, the Action Storehouse (LOG, pp. 77-80) gives a variety of suggestions. Boys should be encouraged to do their best in each of the projects they attempt. A record is kept of each item which gives the date achieved and the number of points earned. As an example, the running project on page 78 gives a boy five points when he runs 50 yards in ten seconds. If he runs the distance in eight seconds, he gets two extra points and a total "score" of seven.

The leader must be alert to situations where there is a background which makes any of the home projects difficult or impossible. Make certain that every boy can complete home projects in some way. When necessary, have Stockade leaders or other men of the church work with boys who either have no parents or whose parents will not help them.

(This section continued in the Appendix at the back, p. 127.)

PIONEER ACHIEVEMENT TRAILS

Brigade Explorer

The first of the Pioneer trails, the Explorer rank is open to any boy who has passed his twelfth birthday, regardless of whether or not he has been active in the Stockade program for younger boys. He is called an Observer until he passes the five tests of strength which qualify him as an Explorer.

Test 1. *Explorer Landmarks* (GUIDEBOOK, pp. 16-18)

a. "Learn and explain the Brigadier's Motto and Watchword and the Explorer's Verse."

"Brigadier's Motto." "Bright and Keen for Christ" should be made very meaningful to every boy in Brigade. The "bright" of the Torch (Matthew 5:14-16, II Corinthians 4:6, Psalm 119:105) and the "keen" of the Sword (Hebrews 4:12, Ephesians 6:17); and the "bright" of a living witness, and the "keen" of a spoken testimony give source material for Battalion Bible studies.

"The Watchword" is the Brigadier's benediction. Use it often, especially at the close of the Battalion meetings.

"Explorer's Verse." John 1:10-12 is one of the best passages in the Word of God for leading a boy to accept the Lord Jesus Christ as his personal Saviour. As a boy comes to his leader to recite the passage, it is natural for the leader to ask, "Do you understand what those verses mean .... can you tell me the name of one person who did receive Him and became a son of God?

b. "Battalion loyalty — be regular in participation and Achievement in Brigade."

Regular attendance at Battalion meetings is defined as attendance of at least three out of every four meetings. Fairness dictates that a boy, to be honored with an advance in rank, must not only meet the specific memory and activity requirements, but must be actively a part of Brigade. Beyond that, in sportsmanship and attitude toward the Battalion as a whole he must be the sort of fellow other Brigadiers can respect. Absence due to illness and such special circumstances can be taken into consideration at the Captain's discretion.

c. "Know the Brigade Hymn and the Seven Points of Valor."

"Brigade Hymn." Each boy's knowledge of this one song will do much for any part of the Battalion program spent in singing. The hymn, or just the chorus, is often used in closing the meeting. Traditionally, Brigade fellows always stand when singing the Brigade Hymn.

"The Seven Points of Valor." The passing of this test requires that a boy know each of the seven points and understand each point's meaning. It is important that the points be interpreted to the boy with such clarity that he can see the personal application to his everyday life. The Scripture portions given in connection with the seven points should be looked up and read by the boy, but neither they nor the explanatory paragraphs in the GUIDEBOOK need be memorized.

1. *Honor.* Honor implies trust. To put a boy on his "honor" is to trust him without question on matters of truthfulness, fairness, and sincerity. A boy who is as good as his word is a living example of honor.

2. *Courage.* Basically, courage is firmness of mind. This firmness permeates the whole attitude of the courageous boy. It is not limited to physical danger; it also embraces difficulties mentally, socially, spiritually. To be courageous does not mean a person cannot experience fear or danger or doubts. But true courage is displayed when one does what is right or necessary *in spite of* the dangers, fears, and doubts.

Here is a good opportunity to use the many vivid stories of courageous boys and men to be found in Scripture and other literature.

3. *Chivalry.* This, the most characteristic of knightly virtues, includes courtesy, manliness, and compassion for those who are weaker and in distress. Chivalry's most important lesson for boys today is the manly respect for womanhood.

However, chivalry should extend to all phases of a boy's life. The good sport, the boy who is considerate of others and is generous in all of his relationships is a better example of chivalry than the fellow who limits his consideration for others only to girls.

4. *Purity.* Purity is necessary in all phases of a boy's life if he is to be healthy. Bodily cleanliness for physical health; mental cleanliness for good health of mind and proper social attitudes; spiritual cleanliness

for serving the Lord — all of these are essentials for the boy who expects to get ahead.

The privilege of the leader is to guide boys from pitfalls which will impair their strength and make them unclean vessels, unfit for the use of the Master.

5. *Loyalty.* The practical tests of loyalty to God, toward which the attention of fellows needs to be turned, concern prayer and faithfulness in Bible reading and study, also church and Sunday School attendance. The point includes, of course, loyalty to Brigade and the Battalion as evidenced by full participation.

6. *Obedience.* To obey is to respect and carry out the expressed desire of another. The Brigade leader who requires a high standard of obedience — wisely and sympathetically — is not only doing a real favor to the boy, but he, in the final analysis, is the only leader who can win and hold the boy's respect and confidence.

7. *Consecration.* Consecration means to set aside or to dedicate for use. A boy who has consecrated his life to the Lord has offered it to Him for service. True consecration cannot be taken lightly.

Never hesitate to spend time on the explanation of this seventh point of valor, and do not hesitate to delay a boy's passing of this test until there is time to really explain all that is involved.

*   *   *   *   *   *   *

The Achievement program is so planned that boys in the Battalion who may have no knowledge of the Word and who are unsaved may be given an opportunity to become active in the program and be won for Christ. The opportune time for a Brigadier to come to know Christ as Saviour — provided he has not come up through the Stockade — is during his days of working for his Explorer rank. The idea of the name is that he is searching or exploring for the truth, and that forms a good basis for the work of the Holy Spirit.

The leader also has the natural opportunity for positive guidance, for a boy working to become an Explorer *comes to him* to explain the Seven Points of Valor, and *comes to him* to recite his passage of Scripture. The leader is in the unique position of not having the barrier between himself and the boy which ordinarily comes in when a man "button-holes" a boy to talk about spiritual things. The opportunity for spiritual guidance afforded is above all other things, natural and unforced.

Test 2. *Strength for Country* (GUIDEBOOK, pp. 18-27)

"Know the Brigadier's code of courtesy to his nation's flag. Correctly execute the fifteen points of Brigade Drill."

Part of "being strong" is to *make strong*. A boy's loyalty to his country, duplicated in the hearts of thousands of others like him, is what makes a nation strong. Loyalty to his flag as the emblem of his country and its people is part of what it takes to be top-notch as a citizen. Being a Christian certainly makes a boy a better citizen, but likewise his being a loyal citizen, carrying readily his share of the load of being one of a great nation of people, brings honor to Christ, and makes that boy a better Christian.

The use of flag ceremonies in the Battalion meeting gives opportunity for correlating instruction in flag lore with the total Brigade program.

In passing a boy on the Flag Code it is not required that he know all the details presented in his GUIDEBOOK. He should know the basic essentials of common flag courtesy. Standard requirement is to know five points under each division (Description of Flag, Proper Manner of Displaying the Flag, and History of the Flag.)

Brigade drill is placed in the Achievement program to give the leader opportunity to tie in some of his regular Battalion activity with the Achievement program. Psychologically, drill will help cement proper discipline for the Battalion and its officers.

These points should be kept in mind in connection with drill:

1. Be sure you know how to execute each point yourself. Act out each one as diagramed in the BOY'S GUIDEBOOK.

2. Help your boys learn the drill by using games such as "Captain Says." Also make use of inter-Squad and inter-Battalion competition and drill teams.

3. Don't make the drill a necessary part of every meeting. The "we must have our drill tonight" idea can easily become a drag on the meeting, especially with older fellows. Once a month emphasis on drill is plenty.

Test 3. *Personal Strength* (GUIDEBOOK, pp. 27-31)

"Obey the requirements of the Explorer's health code, keeping accurate check by means of a chart for a period of one month. Qualify with at least the score of 75 at the end of the month in the Explorer's test of strength and cleanliness."

The requirements of the test for personal strength, with the self-discipline of the daily check-chart, will provide a very real help in the establishment of good standards of personal living among the boys in a Battalion. The Captain's part is to challenge his fellows to keep their charts conscientiously and to enter into their exercises and other activities enthusiastically.

As numbers of boys are keeping their health charts together, it will work out well to plan some special recognition for the boy or boys making the highest score.

The "Seven Muscle Builders" should be used frequently in Battalion meeting during the time when a number of members are working on these tests.

Test 4. *Exploration in the Word of God.* (GUIDEBOOK, pp. 31-39)

"Read — and explore — the Gospel of Mark, one chapter each day for sixteen consecutive days and keep the daily log of reading."

In helping boys with this test it must be remembered that for some of them the Bible will be an entirely new book. Why, after all, read from it? So it is well for the leader to introduce the Bible and its importance. Give some of the historical background, its authors, and an overall picture of its contents.

Captains should be sure to check with boys at least once each week during the sixteen-day period chosen for the reading of Mark, looking over the daily log, making suggestions and offering help in spots where there may be difficulties in understanding. A series of stories like "The Mystery of the Voice from the Wilds" based on the Bible book will be especially meaningful while boys are passing this test.

Test 5. *The Explorer's Adventure* (GUIDEBOOK, p. 40)

"Report on a favorite hobby or activity."

Exploring in hobbies is a forerunner of the wide field of craft endeavor. As the Explorer candidate writes up his hobby and perhaps compares it with those of his chums, he is getting a taste of what he will get into later on when he tackles the work of meeting the requirements for craft certificate Achievement in the fields of his choice.

Several boys may group together on a certain hobby if their individual reports show sufficient originality. On the other hand, the wider the range of hobbies touched, the more interesting the discussion on them will be.

A good feature for a father-son meeting or special program is a hobby show in which each boy puts his hobby on display. All such programs are, of course, most effective if timed to fit the progress of the Brigadiers.

Brigade Trailblazer

The second of the Pioneer trails is open to any boy who has achieved the Explorer rank. He must prove himself in each of the four Trailblazer tests.

Test 1. *Trailblazer Landmarks* (GUIDEBOOK, pp. 42-45)

a. "Know the Brigade Pledge and show your understanding of its meaning by explaining God's way of salvation."

*"Trusting in the Lord Jesus Christ and in Him alone
as my Saviour, I as a Brigadier purpose in my heart to
live bright and keen for Christ that I may glorify Him."*

This test is probably the most basic in the Achievement program. It gives the Battalion leader one of his best opportunities to talk with the individual Brigadier about his relationship to Christ. Through the test the boy comes to the leader to explain to him the way of salvation. It is not necessarily true that a boy must profess acceptance of Christ as his Saviour to pass the test, but he must show his understanding of the way of salvation. The leader talks with him alone and makes sure that he knows. It is also the leader's opportunity to find out where the boy stands personally, and often he has a natural chance to lead an unsaved boy to Christ.

It is very important to avoid giving any boy the idea that the acceptance of Christ is a mechanical thing or part of a test to be passed.

To keep the pledge personal, do not use it in unison.

b. *"Understand and live the Seven Points of Valor."*

Already memorized, and to a certain degree understood by the Explorer, the Seven Points now become themselves a test. The Trailblazer must make them his standard of life.

Re-checking his life as a Brigadier by the Seven Points will be a strengthening practice for every Christian boy, and as man and boy meet for the approval of these tests, the leader will have abundant opportunity to give spiritual guidance and help where needed.

c. *"Know the Story behind Christian Service Brigade and understand its basic organization."* (GUIDEBOOK, pp. 42, 101ff)

A general knowledge of the organization will make a boy's progress in Brigade much more interesting. The history of Brigade and the explanation of its organization are included in his GUIDEBOOK (pp. 42, 101ff). They make good material for quiz programs and tournaments during the Battalion meetings.

Test 2. *Teaching Old Landmarks* (GUIDEBOOK, pp. 45-47)

a. "Your Trailmate"

In the "Trailmate" program is introduced a characteristic phase of Brigade — "bring your buddy." This requirement involves not only bringing in a new boy — perhaps a school friend and often not a Christian — but also sticking with him and helping him to advance in the first of the Pioneer Trails. Normally, trailmates are in the same Squad and the instruction of the Observer takes place as a part of the Squad meeting.

b. "Leadership in Drill"

The "how" of proper drill is in the BOY'S GUIDEBOOK. Snappy correctly executed maneuvers add class to the Battalion. The Sergeant is the key man in all Battalion formations; he, above all, should perfect his ability to give military commands. He should also have a clear understanding of all Battalion formations.

Test 3. *Bible Exploration* (GUIDEBOOK, pp. 47-48)

Encourage boys to start reading the Gospel of John just as soon as they have finished Mark, and then after completing John to start in with Matthew and read the remainder of the New Testament as required for Brigade Guide. The purpose in the sequence of this Bible reading is to get fellows into the chapter-a-day habit, so that regular and careful reading of the Word will become natural to them.

An unsaved fellow studying the Gospel of John as specified in the GUIDEBOOK, marking the word *believe,* should see the plan of salvation throughout his reading. The Christian fellow studying the book will be prepared to help someone else because of that study

The Trailblazer memory verses are especially chosen to be used for leading other fellows to the Lord Jesus.

The Bible Exploration test forms a good foundation for the Brigade Pledge and it can well precede the learning of the Pledge.

Test 4. *Trailblazer Adventure* (GUIDEBOOK, pp. 48-50)

Use the required activities as motivations for general Achievement. Here is a chance to correlate Achievement with activities of especially high boy-interest.

This tie-in has two important aspects. The athletically-minded boy is brought to a keener interest in the program as a whole. Also, Christian boys who may not be well developed in these varying activities—swimming, camping, and team sports—have in this requirement a stimulus for rounding out their experience, which often results in their having a much more effective Christian testimony among other boys.

Physical handicaps which completely bar a boy from accomplishing these athletic tests may be taken into consideration by the Captain, and other types of sports or game participation substituted.

Brigade Guide

The Brigadier who has finished his Trailblazer rank now qualifies to become a Brigade Guide.

In every Battalion there are certain fellows who stand out as more aggressive and more mature than others, and it is quite natural and right that Captains entrust to such boys the bulk of the junior leadership responsibility. It is important, however, to bear in mind that every boy has leadership potentiality. Even the most backward fellow can take the lead in some way in some aspect of his life. As a boy advances to the rank of Guide, he must recognize that higher honor and position in Achievement also involves greater responsibility. To be a Guide involves thinking of and helping other fellows.

The first two of the four Guide requirements are especially significant in light of this emphasis upon leadership training.

Test 1. *The Guide's Landmark* (GUIDEBOOK, pp. 52, 53)

"Study the life of a great Pioneer for Christ, marking well his trail."

Thirty-four great missionary heroes are listed in the BOY'S GUIDE-
BOOK. The study of the lives of these men has inspired many boys
to dedicate their lives to the Lord for missionary service. As a boy
comes to be approved on his reading, encourage him to check over his
own life as to qualifications for doing pioneer work for God on the
foreign or home mission field.

Read these missionary books yourself. They will give you a vision
for your own work, and they'll also provide a vast source of story material
for Council Ring.

Test 2. *Guiding in the Battalion* (GUIDEBOOK, p. 53)

"Plan and lead three consecutive meetings of a Squad of Brigadiers.
Explain the Brigade Pledge to a new Observer in the Battalion."

Here the Guide candidate has opportunity to prove himself in the
most basic aspects of Brigade leadership. In his process of Achievement
through Explorer and Trailblazer he has prepared for this opportunity.
He has taken active part in the full round of Squad activities, has had
experience in teaching the Explorer landmarks to his trailmate, and has
himself learned and explained to his leader the Brigade Pledge.

The planning and leading of the three consecutive Squad meetings
should be done carefully and carried out with the advice of the Captain.
Talk with the boy after the first and second meetings, encouraging him
to think of ways in which he may improve as a Squad leader and make
his meetings better. If the boy is not a Corporal, be sure to clear with
the regular Corporal in the use of his Squad.

In explaining the pledge to a new Brigadier, the Guide candidate is
doing the basic work of Brigade. He is explaining the way of salvation,
perhaps to a boy who has never heard it or who has never accepted
Christ as his own Saviour. If there is no new boy in the Battalion, let
the Guide candidate go out and find one and bring him in.

Test 3. *Bible Exploration* (GUIDEBOOK, pp. 53-55)

"Complete the reading of the New Testament. Memorize the 15 Guide verses. Carefully study a selected book."

Encourage boys to continue their reading in similar fashion to the way they began — reading a chapter a day. They read first the Gospel of Mark, the shortest Gospel and the best for those who may not yet be accustomed to reading the Word. Then they read the Gospel of John, the book which makes clearest, perhaps, the way of salvation. Now they go back to Matthew's Gospel and read through the New Testament. If a boy goes right into the reading of the New Testament within a period of two months after reading Mark and John, he may count these two as already read and continue on into the balance of the New Testament.

Memory work in the verses selected from different books in the New Testament is directly in line with preparation for Christian witnessing and service, because the verses are particularly chosen for their value in doing personal work. Encourage boys also to carry their Testaments in order to show to fellows to whom they may be witnessing just what the Word of God says.

Systematic Bible Study Craft, with requirements as shown in the BOY'S GUIDEBOOK, takes a boy into the careful study of a book of his choice. Encourage your fellows to keep going beyond the first book and study other books as well. The certificate requirements also fit into the preparation of the soul-winner, because they test a boy's ability to turn quickly to any part of the Bible and give from memory a verse of Scripture in answer to key questions that another boy might ask.

Test 4. *Guide's Adventure* (GUIDEBOOK, pp. 55-57)

"Earn three craft certificates and carry out one of the Guide's wilderness expeditions."

Crafts are discussed later in this chapter.

Often fellows will enjoy getting more and more certificates far beyond the requirement of the advancement steps. There is no limit to the number of Brigade Craft Certificates that a boy can achieve if he will keep going. The twelve listed, from which three must be chosen

for this test, were selected to provide a variety of interests with appeal
to boys of different backgrounds.

The expeditions can be made exciting adventure. They do not
require dense forest, in case you have none in your city, but they should
be conducted in some country area away from too much civilization.
Note that expedition "C" requires that the territory be unfamiliar to the
candidate. It should be somewhat new in either of the other two expeditions as well, in order that the required map may actually depend
upon observation at the time and not upon previous knowledge of the
spot in question.

These expeditions can well be taken during the course of a Battalion
or Squad hike. Other boys not advanced as far as the candidates for
this test, staying at the base while the expeditions are in operation, will
be stimulated to work the harder on their own Achievement steps.

ADVANCED ACHIEVEMENT TRAILS

The four specialized advanced trails, Airman, Mariner, Woodsman,
and Ranger, represent specialization in Achievement. They are open only
to boys who are fourteen years or older and have completed the Pioneer
Trails of Explorer, Trailblazer, and Guide.

GENERAL SUGGESTIONS FOR GUIDING FELLOWS ON ADVANCED TRAILS

Before helping a boy on the Advanced Trails, read over each trail
carefully. It's also well to read again the "Suggestions from Cap"
(BOY'S GUIDEBOOK, p. 91).

Boys may enter upon the Advanced Trails singly, advancing at their
own initiative, or they may form a special group working together on a
trail. Sometimes this group will be an already organized Squad. Or it
may be a club made up of boys from several Squads. It is normally
best for the fellows to remain directly associated with the Battalion, because of the need for their leadership and, in turn, their need for leadership opportunity.

Extra meetings of these special squads or clubs can be held by the
Captain or a Lieutenant who has particular ability in the trail being followed.

While the various trails differ on the craft or hobby interest requirements, equal ranks in the trails have the same requirements in these three

tests: Bible Craft Certificate, Bible Study in the Old Testament, and Daily Exercise Chart. What we discuss, then, about these three tests now, applies to all four trails.

The Bible Doctrine crafts follow the outlines in Dr. William Evans' book, GREAT DOCTRINES OF THE BIBLE. (Read carefully the two explanatory paragraphs on page 115 of the GUIDEBOOK in this connection.) Work out with the pastor just what book or instruction he would recommend for the boy as explanation of the truths presented in the outlines. The official teaching of your denomination or individual church, if it is an independent church, can thus be given each boy. Make sure that what is given to them is the *official* position of your church, rather than an individual interpretation.

The Bible study in the Old Testament books follows the method set down in "Some Suggestions from Cap" (BOY'S GUIDEBOOK, p. 93). The leader can do a good deal in introducing the books to the fellows and explaining the applications for today. The written report is required in order to help fellows put Bible truths in their own words and get the basic facts well in mind. These papers should cover the books' main history and 300 to 500 words should be sufficient.

The Daily Exercise Chart, when kept before them as a challenge toward having a good build, will do a lot for boys physically at an age when the right type of exercise can develop them a great deal. Don't let the chart become a chore to be plodded through, but keep it a challenge to physical development. A talk by a Christian athletic coach or a film describing the advantage of exercise can go a long way toward making this requirement popular. Your doing them yourself, will, of course, make as much impression as anything else. They'll help you, too, you know!

Brigade Ranger (GUIDEBOOK, p. 61)

The trail of the Ranger is so named because of the wide range of activities from which to choose. It was given its place in the program of Brigade because it is recognized that boys of this age do not always fit into specialized interest classes.

*Ranger (One Star Ranger)

1. "Master and acquire four new craft certificates from the craft list."

The boy has already earned at least four crafts. The four new ones he now acquires are those he himself chooses from the craft list.

2. "Obtain Bible craft certificate 'Inspiration of the Bible.'"

This craft certificate is awarded the boy who has met the standards outlined on page 115 of the GUIDEBOOK under the section of the Doctrine Crafts outline titled "The Doctrine of the Scriptures."

3. "Range through the Old Testament books of Genesis and Exodus." (Read them!)

A part of this test is the personally worded summary of each book read. (Cap calls it "reconstruction" on page 93 of the GUIDEBOOK.) It will be a big help to the boy to boil down what he got out of his reading.

4. "Keep Daily Exercise Chart for one month."

The "Daily Seven" chart and accompanying suggestions will give you a good start in helping your boys get this requirement. One way to help them be definite in the exercises is to tie them in with the Ranger attainment of well-roundedness.

** Ranger and *** Ranger

These two more advanced ranks in the Ranger trail follow the same pattern as the one-star rank. Time spent in passing the boys on progress up the trail will pay dividends. The boy attaining his three-star rank and going on into Herald work from this Ranger trail will be a well-rounded boy who will normally be excellent leadership material.

Brigade Woodsman (GUIDEBOOK, pp. 62-65)

At the outset of the trail the Brigade Woodsman learns through his Code the reason for his being on this advanced trail: to enjoy the things of creation in the outdoor world; to practice conservation of them; and to prepare himself through these associations to be a witness for the Creator and His plan of salvation. The Woodsman trail is one that will give the boy who follows it the full "how" and "why" of the outdoors.

*Woodsman (One Star Woodsman)

There are nine individual tests. Of these "Identification," "Swimming," "First Aid," "Cooking," and "Knot Tying," are specialized subjects. They require somewhat the same treatment as crafts, and wherever possible should be passed upon by someone qualified in the field. "Bible Crafts," "Bible Reading," and "Exercise Chart" are discussed in the section, "General Suggestions on Guiding Fellows on the Advanced Trails."

**Woodsman and ***Woodsman

These two more advanced ranks in the Woodsman trail follow the same pattern as the one-star rank. In both, one of the large items is the craft assignment. The camping and hiking suggestions in this manual will give the Captain some basic material for the camping and hiking requirements.

Brigade Mariner (GUIDEBOOK, pp. 86-88)

This trail will always have its staunch followers, for the lure of the sea is strong in boys. Returned servicemen with Navy experience can be a big help in the Mariner program, both in the required Mariner crafts and in general program spark.

*Mariner (One Star Mariner)

In this rank the groundwork for Mariner work is laid. A big feature in the requirement is, naturally, the swimming test. Most of the necessary work can be passed by a Captain who has checked the requirements previously. "Bible Crafts," "Bible Reading," and "Exercise Chart" are discussed in the section, "General Suggestions on Guiding Fellows on the Advanced Trails."

**Mariner and ***Mariner

These two more advanced ranks in the Mariner trail follow the same pattern as the one-star rank. There are a number of requirements which a qualified person should pass on, and, of course, craft specialists are needed for the various crafts included in the tests.

Brigade Airman (GUIDEBOOK, pp. 89-91)

In a day when aviation is constantly coming to the fore, the Airman's trail will be the choice of a large number of the fellows when they begin the Advanced Trails. More so than the other three Advanced Trails, Airman, is a highly specialized trail that requires a qualified leader, at least in the craft requirements. The large number of servicemen who have had aviation experience can usually solve the need for such guidance. When you get to the place where some of your gang is ready to go ahead on Airman requirements, check your church or neighborhood for a Christian fellow who has had the necessary experience. There's usually one who is glad to help.

*Airman (One Star Airman)

This rank consists of basic knowledge. If no more qualified person is available, the Captain can guide the boy in the tests by doing a moderate amount of personal research, which, incidently, might prove to be extremely interesting! "Bible Craft," "Bible Reading," and "Exercise Chart" are discussed in the section, "General Suggestions on Guiding Fellows on the Advanced Trails."

**Airman and ***Airman

These two more advanced ranks in the Airman trail follow the same pattern as the one-star rank. Crafts are the major items and here again a qualified guide is necessary.

Throughout the aviation ranks the leader should keep in mind the possibility of a fellow actually making aviation his life work.

THE BRIGADE HERALD (GUIDEBOOK, pp. 98-100)

The earned Achievement rank of Brigade Herald — a Herald of Christ — which requires that a boy have finished the Pioneer Achievement Trails and at least one of the four Advanced Achievement Trails, is the acme of Brigade Achievement. This top rank however does not represent a final pinnacle of Achievement from which every step must be downward, but rather the state of being full-grown as a Brigadier. The Herald has not reached the end of his opportunity for advancement, for ahead of him stretch great and challenging vistas of leadership and service.

The content of the Herald requirements is primarily of the sort to test spiritual strength. Having come thus far through attainment of the various steps of progress in Brigade, the boy has learned to correlate his full round of activities with the things of the Lord and of the Word. No longer is he being tested in these individual activities, but rather on the sum total of what all of these activities have contributed to his spiritual strength and to his usefulness as a servant of Christ.

Of the six tangible Herald requirements, three are concerned directly with the chief general source of leadership training, the Word of God. One requirement asks him to report extensive actual leadership among younger boys, thus applying his training and experience. His written article on Christian living challenges his thinking and helps him to become articulate in the things in which he is growing. Lastly, the very significant daily check chart combines with an organized program for personal devotions to form a strengthening discipline of mind for Christian living.

Herald achievement, the final stretch of a long trail of progress and attainment, clarifies in its nature the great purpose of the entire program from Stockade Builder on up. It is a program of training for Christian service. The boy who has tasted the joy of serving Christ (which he will have done before he has finished this trail of progress), now has before him the continued challenge of joyous service for Him.

CRAFTS IN THE BRIGADE PROGRAM

Crafts are the "fun game of learning about a subject." They are not what is many times called "handicraft work." Boys' interests are as wide as their imaginations, and Brigade crafts are based on this boy interest.

The following pointers will help you get the most out of the craft program for your Battalion. (1) Recognize the big place crafts have in training your boys. (2) Know about the crafts. (3) Have craft guides for as many craft standards as possible. (4) Present craft demonstrations from time to time.

First, recognize the big place crafts have in training boys. Gaining craft certificates actually teaches boys how to have a good time and to be constructive in giving themselves their own recreation. All of the crafts have a definite practical value and some go far in equipping boys to care for themselves, as, for instance, first aid for that accident emergency or woodsmanship for the camping trip. Then there is also the vocational aspect, for good crafts often serve as introductions to what a boy later makes his life vocation. Finally, these activities, by giving useful occupation, further the value of a through-the-week program.

Second, know about the crafts. In relation to your work with the boys, this will equip you to work with all the varied interests of your Battalion. When you have different standards in your mind and can suggest craft helps to your fellows your work will be that much more effective.

Third, have craft guides for as many craft standards as possible. One of the first questions asked by most Captains when they see the 71 craft standards in the BOY'S GUIDEBOOK is, "Do I have to be able to pass boys on all of those?" Of course, you do not. The plan is to have individual men who are qualified in the various fields review boys on their craft standards, which are listed in the BOY'S GUIDEBOOK. Here are a few suggestions on lining up these men as craft guides:

a. Be sure they are Christian men. A man who doesn't know Christ, but who helps a boy in something which leads the boy to admire him, might easily hurt that boy spiritually.

b. Brigade DADS, having already signified their interest in boys by becoming senior members of Brigade, usually make the best guides.

c. Together with your Battalion committee, make up a list of men who are qualified to act as guides on certain crafts. Then talk with each man on the list individually as to his willingness to be a craft guide. Explain that it will not be taking a large portion of his time, but will be a definite contribution to the local Battalion. The boy does all the necessary work on the craft, while the guide directs such work and finally passes on it.

Having obtained a list of available craft guides, it is well to post this list of men (with address and telephone number) and crafts at some convenient place. The boy can then contact the particular craft guide he needs and arrange for working on and passing the craft he has chosen.

d. Be sure to recognize your craft guides as real helpers in your work with the boys, and honor them whenever public reference is made to those working with boys in your church.

Fourth, present craft demonstrations from time to time. One way to do this is to have a craft guide come to the Battalion meeting and give a demonstration during the Captain's Special time. These are good once a month or so, and shouldn't throw the Battalion meeting itself out of balance.

Another type of craft demonstration is the educational movie or film strip. These also fit very well into the Captain's Special time.

ACHIEVEMENT AWARD CEREMONIES

The value of an Achievement award can often be enhanced by the way it is presented. An effective ceremony will serve to make the award itself more impressive and will also leave a lasting effect on the memory of the boy so honored. Be careful, however, to avoid becoming too elaborate or involved, keeping in mind that the important event is the actual award itself.

In the main, there are five different types of meeting during which awards are usually made. They are: regular Battalion meeting; regular church service; special Brigade award meeting in the church; Brigade area rally; and campfire service at a Brigade camp.

Make use as much as possible of committeemen and pastor in the meeting. The actual ceremonies used depend upon the type of meeting and local circumstances. Specific ideas for ceremonies will appear at different times in the Treasury.

CHAPTER OUTLINE

THE BATTALION MEETING

Meeting preliminaries
The meeting schedule
The Battalion Line-up
Squad Meetings
Captain's Special
Battalion Games
Council Ring
The "Non-com" Meeting

BATTALION OUTDOOR ACTIVITY

Camping
Hiking

BATTALION ATHLETICS

BATTALION PROGRAM PLANNING

THE STOCKADE IN ACTION

Stockade Posts
Stockade Council Meeting

CHAPTER SIX

Battalion in Action

THE BATTALION MEETING

Meeting Preliminaries

a. PLACE. The church building or Christian Education building is by far the best place for the meeting. This ties the club closer to the church. If the church does not have the facilities for a meeting place on its own property, a rented hall or, if necessary, gymnasium will do. Keep as close to the church center as possible.

b. DAY. No set statement can be made as to the day for the meeting. Every night of the weekdays has been used successfully when fit in with the local circumstances. The night of the big high school basketball or football games in smaller towns, and city-wide youth activities in larger places must be considered. A big item always, of course, is clearing with your own local church calendar.

c. TIME. Time for beginning the meeting will vary in different places. Evenings are better than afternoons because of school athletics and afternoon work. Set the earliest possible time that all the leaders and boys can be on hand. In many places this is seven o'clock. However, in some sections it is necessary to start at seven-fifteen or even seven-thirty. It *is* important to set a time which is always the same and to actually start at that time. The schedule given here assumes the starting time as seven-thirty. The Sergeant should be on hand fifteen minutes early.

The Meeting Schedule

The standard Battalion meeting, used almost without exception wherever Brigade is in operation, follows two paradoxical general requirements: It must always be the same; it must never be the same! The skeleton framework of the meeting is standard. However little or much they themselves may contribute to order, all boys want their meeting to be orderly. But within the bounds of the framework there is packed a

69

wealth of variety — there is always something new at a good Battalion meeting.

A TYPICAL BATTALION MEETING PROGRAM

7:15 - Sergeant on hand to be sure meeting place is in shape and to direct *informal games*, contests, and activities among the early comers. Officers also on hand to pass Achievement tests, especially for Corporals. A brief pre-meeting confab with junior leaders to check program for meeting.

7:30 *"Battalion Fall In!"* Sergeant in charge. Meeting begun with prayer.

7:35 - *Squad meetings.* Corporals in charge.

7:50 - Squads report. Sergeant takes the report from each Corporal on the Squad's attendance and progress,then reports the total Battalion attendance to the Captain.

7:55 - *"Captain's Special."* Ten minutes of something brand new in the way of Battalion activity, with special emphasis on Achievement.

8:05 - *Battalion games.* Kept lively by variation and change. Games worked in natural sequence into Council Ring.

8:40 - *Council ring.* The time when a message is brought from the Word of God to the fellows, usually in story form. Direct invitations are not usually given, but the fellows are encouraged to stay after dismissal to chat about problems or questions.

9:00 - *Battalion dismissed* with the Brigade Watchword, possibly the singing of the Brigade Hymn.

9:05 - Short meeting of Corporals and Sergeants with the Captain to discuss the success of the meeting, to note how it could be improved, to work on the non-coms own Achievement (they should be ahead of the rest of the Battalion), and most especially to pray together.

The Battalion Line-up

The king-pin in the Battalion line-up and in keeping things running smoothly in the Battalion meeting is the Sergeant. This section is written from his slant, and is here for the Captain to understand and work over with his Sergeant.

(1)   "Fall in . . . Battalion, Atten*tion!*

Captain and Sergeant are early for the meeting. After the non-com meeting and during the period before the opening of the Battalion meeting proper, individual contests like Indian wrestling, horse fights, and games that work well with comparatively few, are organized (See Treasury). At the time when the meeting is scheduled to begin, the Captain speaks to the Sergeant instructing him to call up the Battalion. Sergeant commands, *"Fall in!"* Then, allowing a moment for the Corporals to line up their Squads, he gives the preparatory command, "Battalion . . ." The Corporals facing their Squads give the preparatory command simultaneously, "Squad . . . then the Sergeant gives the command of execution sharply: "Atten*tion!*"

Sergeant and Corporals are standing at attention themselves, but they are checking the lines to be sure that the line is perfect.

(2)   "Corporals, posts!"

When satisfied with the line-up, the Sergeant commands: "Corporals, take your posts!" The Corporals, who have been facing their Squads, each one centered on his Squad line at a distance of two paces from the line, take one step forward toward the Squad lines and execute *about face.* They stand at attention facing the Captain.

If any boy in line breaks attention and causes disturbance in the line, he is never corrected by the Sergeant or by the Captain or Lieutenant directly. The Sergeant calls the offender's Corporal on it. The Corporal is directly responsible for the Squad discipline.

(3)   "Battalion is formed, Sir!"

Satisfied with the entire Battalion line-up, the Sergeant executes *about face* and salutes the Captain. Holding the salute he reports: "Battalion is formed, Sir!" He continues to hold his salute until the Captain returns it, which should be as soon as the Sergeant has finished reporting. The instant the Captain salutes, the Sergeant drops his hand to his side and stands at attention awaiting instructions.

(4)   "Sergeant, post!"

The Battalion formed, the line checked by Corporals and Sergeant and reported ready by the Sergeant, the Captain says: "Sergeant, post!" The Sergeant executes *left face* and marches to his post even with the end of the line, and on a line with his original post in the center of the room.

In this formation the Captain is in charge, directly, of the Battalion in line. This is the formation to be used for making announcements by the Captain or other commissioned officers. At this point in the meeting, having received the report from the Sergeant that the Battalion is formed, the Captain commits the Battalion and its meeting to the Lord. He gives the command, *"Parade rest"* and leads very briefly in prayer.

After the brief prayer, if a flag ceremony is used it comes here with the Sergeant in charge. The Captain then makes any announcements concerning the evening program that he wants made before Squad meetings. For instance, he may announce: "There will be a tournament following Squad meetings, testing on the Seven Points of Valor and the flag code. The winning Squad will be taken to the Zilchtown Zoo tomorrow!" Thus, added impetus might be given for concentrated study during Squad meetings.

(5)   "Corporals, take your Squads into Squad meetings!"

After announcements the Captain turns to the Sergeant and says, "Dismiss to Squad meetings." The Sergeant salutes from his post, then marches to his original post in the middle of the room and commands: "Corporals, take your Squads into Squad meetings!" Immediately the Corporals take charge of their Squads and direct them to whatever place the Squad meeting is held. Although the illustration shows four Squads meeting in four corners of one room, it is far better for each Squad to have a small room of its own, whenever it is workable for it to be arranged. In the privacy of a separate room it is possible to build better Squad unity and to make more progress as a Squad.

During Squad meetings the Corporal is entirely in charge. The Sergeant may come in to make announcements or to obtain information, but he does not interrupt the Corporal and waits for opportunity to speak. If a commissioned officer comes into a Squad meeting, the Corporal immediately calls the Squad to attention and he himself salutes the officer. When an officer does not wish to interrupt (i.e., at all times except when he is testing them for Squad courtesies), he says "rest" or "carry on" before the Corporal has a chance to call up his Squad.

The Sergeant is in charge of the Battalion during Squad meetings in that he is responsible for late comers and boys passing in and out of Squad meetings (for tests only). Newcomers arriving during Squad meetings are brought by the Sergeant and introduced to the Captain. Members arriving late are dispatched by the Sergeant to the proper Squad meeting.

Boys ready to pass Achievement tests are sent during Squad meetings to the Captain or one of the Lieutenants, who should normally spend most of this time in conference with individual boys. If one officer is not thus occupied, he may inspect the Squads. He does not remain long on any one Squad meeting nor does he in any way take the authority in the meeting away from the Corporal in charge.

If a Corporal is absent, his Lance Corporal automatically is vested for the time being with all of the responsibilities and authority of a Corporal. It is the responsibility of a Corporal to notify his Lance Corporal if it is ever necessary for him to be absent.

(6) "Squads, *report!*"

The Sergeant is responsible for helping carry out the Battalion program according to schedule. If there is a bugler, the Sergeant instructs him when to blow various calls. (A whistle is a good substitute.) When it is time for Squad meetings to terminate, the Sergeant calls immediately for Battalion line-up and reports to the Captain when the Battalion is formed as in points (1), (2), and (3). At this time, instead of instructing the Sergeant to take his post, the Captain instructs him: "Take the report of the Squads." The Sergeant salutes, executes *about face,* and commands: "Squads, *report!*" The Corporal of the Squad furthest to the Captain's left reports first. Each of the other Squads reports in turn. The Sergeant keeps track of the total attendance as he goes along. When all the Squads have reported, he executes *about face* and salutes the Captain, reporting: "Battalion (whatever number) reporting, Sir, (whatever number) present." The Sergeant holds the salute until it is returned.

Then comes Captain's Special, the variable program feature which often includes a special surprise, and usually sparks Achievement in some way. The Captain or one of his Lieutenants generally takes care of this feature.

(7) "Line formation, Fall in!"

Captain's Special over, there follows Game Time. Many good Battalion games like "Steal the Bacon" and "Pom-Pom Pullaway" require numbering off from one long line when Squads are not used as teams. For such purpose the Battalion line formation is used. Corporals and Sergeants are the only ones who have a different position from that in the report formation. Each Corporal stands at the head of his Squad line to the right of his Lance Corporal, and the Sergeant stands at the head of the Battalion line at the right of the first Corporal.

When the Sergeant gives Line formation, the Battalion lines up with the first Corporal as guide and after they have fallen in, he takes his own place in line. When the command is given by an officer, the Sergeant takes his place but faces down the line to check the straightness of the line, then executes right face and remains in place.

During the Game Time and the Council Ring which follows, the Sergeant mixes in with the rest of the fellows. He has a good time that way and also increases his influence with the rest of the gang.

After Council Ring the Sergeant should watch for opportunity for personal work with individual fellows who may not know Christ as their Saviour. Oftimes a new boy coming into the Battalion will be too timid to go to one of the leaders, but since the Sergeant is one of the fellows, he will come to him instead. Here is his chance to witness to the new boy for the Lord Jesus.

During the short non-com meeting after the Battalion meeting, the Sergeant gives his ideas to the Captain on how the whole meeting could have gone better, and also makes suggestions to the Corporals on how they each could have done better in their Squads. Coming from him, these suggestions will mean a lot if they are given in the right way, respectfully and straight forwardly.

Squad Meetings

Key man in Squad meetings is the Corporal. Like the previous section for the Sergeant, this section is written from the Corporal's slant, and is to be worked over with him.

1. The Squad takes its bearings

Where's the Squad going? What will it try to accomplish? Here are some practical ideas on the direction a live-wire Squad ought to be heading.

(a) Build the unity of the Squad with Achievement teamwork, through-the-week activity, and increasing friendships. (b) Help each member of the Squad to grow stronger: in his Christian life, and in his physical strength; in his keeness of mind; and in his own teamwork as a member of the Squad. (c) Strive to make the Squad the top in the Battalion. Each new Brigadier brought by a Squad member automatically belongs to that Squad.

Brigade Achievement will give the "how" for these objectives. Full of action and accomplishment, the various ranks and tests will keep each Squad on its toes and growing. So, one of the best, easiest, and most practical ways for a Squad to work toward its aims is to go heavy on Achievement. A part of the Squad program should be to have every member advancing regularly. A certain date, for instance, can be set by which members will try to finish their Explorer requirements. The Corporal must be sure to keep ahead of the others.

A good way to build unity and teamwork and Squad loyalty is through competition with other Squads. One Squad challenges another Squad to a ball game, or in Battalion meetings to some other sort of game like "Steal the Bacon" or "Blackout." Competition can be had in drill contests, too, or in any number of different contests based on Achievement requirements, such as "Seven Muscle Builders." In the Achievement contests two birds will be killed with one stone — making headway with Achievement, and building Squad teamwork by competition.

Squad outings, hikes, overnight camping trips, and trips to parks, museums, and exhibits are also good Squad builders.

Another phase of Squad activity might be labelled Squad secrets. A special code, whistle, handshake, password, or insignia, known only to the Squad members is always a lot of fun. Also, there can be Squad songs, Squad cheers, Squad emblems, and other individual Squad material.

2. The Squad Name

Each Squad should have a good name — one that sounds snappy when shouted. Some names in the past have been Crusaders, Rough Riders, Rangers, Commando, Iron Guard, Eagles, Bulldogs, Prospectors, Badgers, Model T's, Fearless Frogs, Golden Gophers, Golden Cobras, Blue Bats, Tigers, Flaming Swords, David's Mighty Men, Knights of Gideon, Thunderbolts, Silver Trumpets, Wildcats, Golden Shields, Flying Arrows.

3. Weekly Squad meetings

The fifteen minutes immediately following the opening formation are Squad time. During that time the Corporal is in full charge of the Squad and it is his job to see that the fellows get their full fifteen minutes' worth of action and accomplishments.

(a) Squad Devotions. The first few moments of Squad time are used to commit the meeting to the Lord. The Corporal or one of the fellows reads several verses from the Bible and there's the short time of prayer and sometimes singing of a chorus or one of the Brigade songs.

(b) Squad Achievement. Most of the remaining time is spent in the main job of the Squad meeting, namely, helping the fellows to pass their Achievement tests. The Corporal should test each fellow individually on each test passed and when satisfied that he is ready to pass it officially, send him out to the Captain or Lieutenant. Battalion commissioned officers are standing by during the Squad meetings ready to pass fellows on their Achievement tests. Every test to be officially passed must be initialed in the BOY'S GUIDEBOOK or Achievement chart by a commissioned officer.

(c) Squad Planning. The closing moments of the Squad meeting are spent in conference concerning future activities, plans, and Squad challenges. Every one should take part with ideas and suggestions.

(d) Squad Shares. Shares are collected during the Squad meeting. One week's shares each month are set aside as missionary funds. The other shares are used for the Battalion's own expenses.

4. The Corporal in Squad Formations

It is important for every Corporal to handle himself properly in all Squad and Battalion formations. At the beginning of each Battalion meeting, when the Sergeant is preparing to call the Battalion up to attention, he forewarns the Corporals, "Corporals, call up your Squads." Immediately each Corporal calls his Squad members from whatever they are doing to prepare for the line-up.

When the Sergeant gives the preparatory command, "Battalion. . ." each Corporal passes it on to his charge saying, "Squad . . ." Then the Sergeant alone gives the command of execution, "Atten*tion!*"

At the beginning of the line-up the Corporal stands in front of the center of his line, facing his Squad, two paces from the line. While he is facing them he is directly in charge. When the Sergeant commands, "Corporals, posts," each Corporal immediately takes one step forward toward his line, stops, and executes *about face*. Now he is facing the Sergeant or Captain and is on the alert for whatever is to go on next.

At the end of the Squad meetings, the Battalion forms exactly as at the beginning of the meeting. Now, after the Sergeant reports to the Captain that the Battalion is formed, the Captain instructs him to take the report of the Squads. The Sergeant then executes *about face* and commands, "Squads, report!" The Squad furthest to the Sergeant's left reports first, and then one after another reports right down the line. The report is as follows:

Corporal faces straight forward (does not turn to face Sergeant). His report might be: "Crusader Squad reporting, Sir; eight present; 88 cents, shares; we reviewed the Seven Points of Valor and three fellows passed their test; we made final plans for our hike to Hickory Creek." The Corporal includes himself in his attendance report for his Squad. After each of the Corporals has reported, the Sergeant reports for the entire Battalion, giving the total attendance, including himself. The important things about the phrasing of the Corporal's report are the first two statements; the standard form should be used: "(name) Squad reporting, Sir; (number) present." Then he goes on to give in brief the accomplishments of the Squad during the evening's meeting.

5. Squad Discipline

No Corporal should tolerate disorder during Squad meetings. His badge of authority is the loyalty of his Squad members   He will point out to the fellow not cooperating that he is hurting the Squad as a whole. If a fellow remains rebellious, he is sent to the Captain.

Captain's Special

Right into the middle of the evening's Battalion meeting is injected a surprise time, a part of the program which is never quite the same from week to week. Used wisely, it can be the Captain's most effective means of sparking the Achievement program.

Two tested features for Achievement push are the Tournament and the Confab. In the Tournament there is general competition in answering questions aimed at the basic parts of the Achievement program. A Squad champ is chosen who takes on all challengers until dethroned.

In the Confab the Battalion breaks up into small groups that work on different Achievement tests under an advanced leader. Both the Tournament and the Confab are given in detail in the Treasury. Read the directions there before attempting to use either feature.

Somewhat along the lines of the Tournament are the marching drill, calisthenic contest, and general drill.

Sometimes the Confab will be preceeded (or replaced if necessary) by a featured presentation of a certain test. Thus, for instance, the Captain could introduce the reading of the Gospel of Mark with a talk on the Bible, its history, contents, or importance.

Another good Captain's Special idea is the scheduling of craft demonstrations, such as first aid, aircraft recognition, nature lore. The use of moving pictures and slides, available from various sources, can be a valuable part of such demonstrations.

Mixed in with these educational specials should be some plain *fun* features. A circus, for example, where each Squad plans a stunt for the entertainment of the others, is a good standby. Fun stories, pie-eating contests, and similar ideas, when not overworked, do much to make Captain's Special a looked-for part of the program.

Battalion Games

Games are an important part of the Battalion meeting. They are not in the program just to take up time, but they have a definite, planned purpose. The Captain who gets the most out of his Game Time knows not merely the games themselves, but also the purposes behind them and how to accomplish those purposes.

WHY GAMES ARE IN THE BATTALION PROGRAM

(1)   Every boy likes to play.   Hence, good games have great appeal to boys.   That is one legitimate reason for using them.   Game Time is a part of the program everyone will thoroughly enjoy, and when boys are having a good time the opportunities for reaching them increase. Also, the appeal of games affords the fellows an opportunity to bring their friends, who may have no interest whatever in the spiritual things of the Battalion meeting, and guarantee them a lot of fun.

(2)   Games form one of the best possible ways for a leader to get to know his boys.   There are two distinct ways in which this is true. In the first place, games overcome barriers of strangeness.   Playing together begets friendliness, and the man who can enter in and play with boys and really enjoy it is quick to earn their friendship.   Besides that, a leader can get to know a great deal about boys in general and about individual boys in particular just by watching them play.   Oftimes he will learn more about the leadership, intelligence, adaptability, perseverance, probable faithfulness, and general qualifications of his fellows by watching them play games for a half-hour or so than by talking with them for a good deal longer.

For a test of boys' mental alertness, for instance, games like "Steal the Bacon," "Rhythm," "Get Herman," and "Spoof" are very revealing. Of these, "Steal the Bacon" and "Spoof" are also very good for both testing and developing self-control.

For physical robustness and strength — which have a definite correlation to boy leadership — games like "American Eagle," "Blackout," "Poison," and "Horse Fighting" test both strength and stamina.   Physical coordination and skill are well tested by "Dodge Ball" and "Spin the Rope."

All games test sportsmanship, a necessary quality for good leadership. It doesn't take long in short games like these mentioned to find out who is a good winner and a good loser and who is not.

The quality of moral fortitude — the ability to "take it" — is a priceless quality in leadership. "Swat" games like "Who am I?" and "Swat Tag" reveal a lot about a fellow in that way.

It is very readily recognized that games do not provide a leader with a whole picture of a boy. Yet, in how he plays the game, a boy reveals his physical and mental strength, and most especially, his social nature. These things in very great degree show the practical outworking of his Christian life within.

(3)   A rather different phase of the use of games is the aspect of games used as actual means of training. Just as it was mentioned that "Spoof" and "Steal the Bacon" not only test but help to develop self-control, so many of these games become powerful means whereby a leader can bring about a change in the lives of his boys through play-training. An example of this is the positive discipline in the game of "Steal the Bacon." In a group of boys who may be rather noisy and inclined to run uncontrolledly about the meeting hall, this game requires that every fellow stand in a definite place in line listening quietly for a number. The stimulus to fit in, to stay in line, and to be quiet is in this case group-approval. If one boy doesn't cooperate, he ruins the game for his team— and usually hears about it. Thus, there are a number of definite ways in which the playing of games has practical value for character building and leadership training.

Games also help to overcome adolescent clumsiness. Through games requiring physical coordination and control, growing boys are helped to develop out of their natural awkwardness.

Games help to train and develop boys' natural talents. Skills of various sorts, mental as well as physical, are developed by the using. Many games require the use of accuracy of aim, ability to concentrate, quickness of reaction.

Games, and especially team games, help to develop group leadership. The boy who can effectively pep up his team and spur them on to greater effort while playing hard right with them is himself demonstrating some of the most essential qualities of leadership.

Learning to be thoughtful of others is a very prevalent need among boys. The give-and-take of games, together with the positive discipline of realizing that a game has to be played right in order to be worthwhile, make definite steps in that direction.

(4) The greatest purpose for the prominence of games in the weekly Battalion meeting is something beyond all the values already mentioned. *Games in the Battalion meeting are a preparation for the bringing of the spiritual message in Council Ring.* This vital point is fully explained under the next heading.

How To Use Games In The Battalion Meeting

One method of classifying games in two groups identifies one group as "games of confusion," and the other as "games of order." "Games of confusion" are those that do not involve any closely defined formation — you "play all over the floor." Such games are "American Eagle" and "Blackout." "Games of order," on the other hand, require definite lines or circles either standing, like "Swat Tag" or sitting in chairs like "Spoof" or "Rhythm." Both classifications consist of active games. Some require more physical exertion, others more mental concentration.

In the Battalion meeting game sequence, "games of confusion" come first. They are also usually the games that take the most physical energy; games that give the fellows a chance to blow off steam. From these the sequence goes naturally into "games of order." "Steal the Bacon" has even lines, but still plenty of physical action. "Spoof" is still more ordered — an even circle of chairs — but again involves considerable physical action.

The final games invariably have the fellows sitting in a circle and possibly exerting more mental than physical energy. Then, without any break in the sequence of interest, the Captain begins a story. The story carries a straight-from-the shoulder message from the Word of God. And the message is not hidden, but it is brought in right on the plane where it belongs — the plane of things vitally interesting to boys.

In practical outworking, this principle of games leading up to the Council Ring as the climax of the meeting has proved to be tremendously effective. Any activity into which a boy may enter as a Christian need not be separated from spiritual matters. Therefore to go from Brigade game activity into talking about Christ ought always to be in place.

The passing from Game Time to Council Ring is a natural sequence. The reason, however, for going from games of high physical activity to those of more mental energy prior to the Council Ring might need explanation. For one thing, restlessness, which is so frequent with boys, is invariably the result of over-stimulated, or else under-exercised, nervous energy. When a fellow's body is tense and when his nervous reactions are keyed to a high pitch (as will be the case after the playing of some of the more energetic Battalion games), to expect him then to suddenly sit down and convert immediately to mental energy and attention, is to work against the boy's natural impulses. Hence, mental games bridge the gap. Also, the use of those games which stimuate mental alertness prepares the boy to think. And the message of the Word of God, brought in dependence upon the Holy Spirit to the minds of thinking boys, will bear fruit.

CHOOSING THE GAMES

We have considered something of the sequence of games and the general classifications of "games of confusion" and "games of order." To put this into practice, a foundation list of typical games for Battalion use are given in the "Game Bag" in the Treasury. However, every alert Captain is constantly on the lookout himself for ideas that can be made into new games, and it may be helpful here to set down some of the requirements for a good Battalion game.

(1) *Action.* There is plenty of action in a good Battalion game. The game must move fast. Few of the sort of games in which only some of the players are active fit into Battalion use. The action should be such that every player is challenged by the game to put his full energy into it, regardless of whether it be primarily physical or mental activity.

(2) *Object.* A game that goes over with boys must have a distinct and attainable objective reachable in the immediate action of the game. It should be a challenging objective.

The playing of the game is struggling to obtain the objective as quickly as possible, whether it be to amass a certain number of points, as in

"Steal the Bacon"; to eliminate all the players on the other team, as in "Dodge Ball"; to get every player onto one team as in "American Eagle"; or to be last one in the game as in "Spin the Rope." Successful games usually have a definite winner, either individual or team.

(3) *Suspense.* The uncertainty of outcome that results from adequate challenge and balanced competition is a big part of a game's success. "Spoof" is a good example, where everyone has a chance, but the winner is not determined until one of the two last players is eliminated.

(4) *Participation.* Good Battalion games allow for full participation for any number of players, so that all the fellows can be actively taking part in all of the games. When a boy has to sit down and watch he doesn't enjoy the game as much as when he is in it. One problem that is introduced by this point and needs watching is the situation in elimination games where the players drop out one by one. Half way through the game there are apt to be more fellows watching than playing. If they are disorderly, it will disturb the game and disrupt the meeting. Games that have a high spectator interest often solve the problem, and team spirit also helps.

(5) *Suited to Age Group.* For the most part, the popularity of a game among both older and younger boys depends not so much on the game itself as upon the way it is introduced and led. Nevertheless, there are certain types of games that are only best for younger boys, and others that are primarily older fellows' games. But in the Battalion there is often quite a marked age variance. "Steal the Bacon" and "American Eagle" are notably good for use with boys of mixed ages within the Battalion range. "Poison," on the other hand, gives all the advantages to bigger fellows. Where physical strength is a big factor, it is sometimes a good idea to run two games at once, dividing according to height.

Above all, do not try to use games with older fellows which to their own minds, for one reason or other, will be regarded as "kid stuff."

How To Lead Games

(1) The most important single factor in the success of games as a feature of any boys' activity program is the *spark* with which those

games are presented and led. Enthusiasm, good humor, and snap are the chief characteristics of effective game leadership. The leadership itself should be spread among the leaders of the Battalion. Captains, Lieutenants, and even the non-coms should have a definite game contact. Individual leaders often become especially adept in leading certain games.

(2) *Plan* the Game Time well, choosing games thoughtfully in advance. Do not allow Game Time to become a free-for-all of each boy's shouted game suggestion. Introduce new games frequently. Don't overdo a game that is well liked, and seldom play the same game in successive meetings. In some places of meeting there are limitations which make certain games impractical, but don't be afraid to play good active games even in close quarters. "Spoof" can be played anywhere; "Poison" nearly everywhere. In very large rooms (gymnasiums, halls, and the like) it is important to keep the unity of the game period. .

There are two times in the Battalion meeting that games are used. In the period before the meeting actually begins, "informal" games are used. These are any type of game that can be played with from two or three players up to a half-dozen or more. They have no necessary duration so that they can be cut into easily and without delay at the time that the line-up is due. The main time for games in the Battalion, however, is the regular game period lasting around a half-hour, just prior to Council Ring time.

Plan the order of the games with the principle of sequence in mind and also with thought as to smoothness in going from one game to the next. Arrange games so that each game played involves a quite different activity from the one played just before it.

Before the start of the Battalion meeting the game leader should have a written list of the games to be played in the order of the playing, yet the introduction of each game should be casual and spontaneous lest the meeting seem to the boys to be "canned."

When plans have been made prayerfully and with thought as to what will make the most effective and enjoyable Battalion get-together, stick to the plans and carry them out. True, unforeseen circumstances or ideas may come up and you will want to adjust to meet them, but do so with your basic plan in mind.

(3) *Know* your games. It is important for the game leader to be very well acquainted with the game he is leading, to know all the rules (a good game has a minimum), and to know all the problems that may arise in the game. If the game requires equipment, he should be on hand with the equipment. The effective leader of boys' games wins the confidence and cooperation of the fellows by *knowing his stuff and by being prepared to play the game.*

In nearly every group of boys there is at least one who knows how to play a game " a better way" now and then. The answer to that is, "Good, be sure to tell me about your way later — but this time we will play it this way to see how it works..." It is important to follow through with the game as planned for the sake of unity and smoothness in the program. Always take advantage of the ideas boys have about games. They are in some degree authorities on what things boys like, and you may get some really good suggestions.

A practical idea for new Battalion leaders is this. Get your non-coms together for a special pow-wow and go through all the games in the Treasury; figure each one out; and actually play it. You will avoid coming before the Battalion with a game you have never led or seen played, and you will also have another valuable personal contact with your non-coms.

(4) *Explain* new games thoroughly and clearly. When introducing a new game, it should only be necessary to explain it once, but that should be done in a loud clear voice with the ample use of demonstration. Do not tolerate any inattention during the time of explaining a game, and avoid tiresome repetition. Anticipate confusion or questions the fellows will have and cover them in your explanation. Once the boys catch on to the game, get right into it without further delay.

(5) *Move* right along. Streamline your game period by avoidance of interruptions and delays. Forethought in little things will greatly facilitate this. Much time can be saved by being sure to have the equipment necessary for the game handy to be used at the moment it is needed. Often it works out rather well when a Captain and Lieutenant alternate in leading games. While one is leading the other can be preparing for the game to follow. If the Captain is leading the Council

Ring, the Lieutenant would probably lead the last game and thus allow
the Captain time to get set to move right into Council Ring.

(6) *Change* games frequently in the course of the game period.
As soon as one game begins to get to be a lot of fun, quiet it and play
another one. It is much better to stop a game while the fellows are
really enjoying it than to wait 'till it begins to be tiresome. The game
that is changed at the peak of its interest is "kept hot" for use at a future
meeting.

(7) *Enforce* positive standards of sportsmanship. Behavior should
be disciplined. If it is a minor matter of disturbance, it may suffice to
request a boy to sit out the rest of the game. The question of discipline
is taken up fully later. Most important of all right here is the point
that under no circumstances should the whole group have to be unduly
disrupted by the misbehavior of one boy. After the leader has asked
a boy to sit down and wait until the game is over, he immediately goes
on with the game with just as much enthusiasm as before.

One problem occasionally occurring, especially with younger boys,
is the question of what to do when a boy gets hurt in playing a game. If
there is any serious injury — an extremely rare circumstance in a Brigade
game period, but one for which every leader should be ready — the
Captain or other mature person present will want to give his full attention
to the injured boy, but the Game Time should go on uninterrupted, as
much for the sake of the boy who is hurt as for the unity of the meeting.
A Lieutenant takes over the game, or, in the absence of a Lieutenant,
the Sergeant.

(8) In your planning, *tune* your games to the meeting as a whole.
When your plans are written up on paper, look them over. Determine
whether or not the games fit into the program to make a smooth, unified
whole. Do Captain's Special, Game Time, and Council Ring fit together?
Will the sequence of games do what you want it to do in the way of
preparing the boys for the message or discussion of the Council Ring?
If so, your planning of games is complete.

Council Ring

Council Ring is the climax of the Battalion meeting. The well-
planned program has prepared for this time and leads naturally into it

Council Ring gives opportunity for presenting a message to the fellows. There are two general aspects of the message to be presented: informational — guiding boys in the understanding of the truths of the Word of God; inspirational — leading boys to interpret those truths in practical terms in their everyday living.

Regardless of the emphasis of your message, it will revolve about the person of Jesus Christ. He and His work are the underlying basis of all that Council Ring seeks to accomplish. Whether directly or indirectly, keep Christ in the thought of the message.

THE LEADER OF COUNCIL RING

Normally Council Ring should be led by the Captain of the Battalion. At times Lieutenants will take active part in it as well. In both cases Council Ring time is being led by the men who have directed the other parts of the program also. This is as it should be, for they are the established leaders whose teaching and spiritual guidance in this part of the program will be accepted as such.

Occasionally the pastor or an outsider may be used to lead Council Ring. In that case he should be urged to enter into as much of the meeting as possible. The more he is associated with the fellows the more he will have their confidence and interest when he talks to them of spiritual things.

PREPARATION FOR COUNCIL RING

In preparing for Council Ring, the leader does not first study the Bible for a good message and then look around for boys to spring it on. Rather, he studies the Word prayerfully with the needs of his boys in mind, asking the Lord to guide him in finding the truths which are best suited to the boys' individual needs.

In the formative days of many Battalions, the primary spiritual need among the fellows is the need of salvation. To such fellows the Council Ring's greatest purpose will be presentation of the facts of salvation. The greater part of leading boys to definite decisions, however, will normally come in individual personal work. After most of the boys in the gang have taken a definite stand for Christ, the leader of Council Ring will be vitally concerned with using the time for meeting the needs of the growing Christians.

The three-fold need of every Christian should be kept in mind in the planning for Christians: food — understanding the truth of the Word; breath — communion with God in prayer; exercise — witnessing for the Lord in daily living.

When a story is on the docket — the story is the main type of message the leader will use — the Council Ring leader in preparing will think first about the spiritual instruction or inspiration toward which the story is to be directed.

Many a man has faced his time of preparation for Council Ring with a feeling of inadequacy for the job. It is well to remember that the Lord has promised the necessary abilities for presenting His Word. That man is best qualified to lead boys to Christ through the message of a Battalion Council Ring who trusts neither to his own ability to tell a story or hold boys' attention nor to his own understanding of the deep things of God. But he is prepared who faithfully does his part and then leans wholly on the Lord.

GETTING THE MESSAGE ACROSS

Guiding boys in Council Ring towards an understanding of the Word of God cannot be done by traditional teaching method. Studies in a certain book of the Bible continued as such from week to week are in most cases ineffective for Council Ring. The teaching sequence must be functional, following logically the spiritual growth of the boys.

The leader — or teacher — should first master the particular truth to be used as taught in the Bible. He must think it through until he understands it in thought and not only in words. Then, putting himself in the position of the fellows, he must seek to interpret those thoughts into the realities of boys' understanding and terminology.

There are, generally speaking, three types of Council Ring presentation, each with its particular value in teaching the Word.

First, there is the STORY. It is the most frequently used; and with younger boys, it is used almost exclusively. The normal boy has a rather short attention span, making it difficult for him to follow, for instance, a complicated outline. A story message overcomes this in that it is characteristic of any good story to carry all of its facts right along with it in the development of its plot. Whereas boys may *listen* to an ordinary message, they *live* in a story, and the facts stick.

Second, there is the DISCUSSION. It is used occasionally, especially with older fellows. When fellows take part themselves in the Bible-exploring time their interest is increased and maintained.

Last, we have the STRAIGHT TALK, which can be used under certain circumstances. Now and then it can be varied by the use of object lessons, gospel magic, and chalk illustrations.

TELLING STORIES TO BOYS

Good story-telling is a valuable talent for a boys' leader, a talent which a little honest effort and practice will in most cases readily develop.

(1) The Story Itself.

Beginning. The Council Ring story begins with action. Where an introduction may be necessary, it will be brief. Get the boys' attention and interest with the very first sentence.

Plot. The plot is the main body of the story. It is a series of events moving in succession, each creating the next. Each event, though an inseparable part of the story, has great interest in itself.

Climax. The climax is the real reason for telling the story. All events lead to it. Until it is reached there is a sense of mystery or suspense. The truth you are putting across will be in the climax.

Ending. A bungling close can entirely spoil an otherwise good story. Once the climax has been reached, the ending follows quickly without being dragged out in any way. A well-worded sentence is often sufficient.

In general, be sure the story hangs together. Every detail of a good story contributes something to the plot. Be careful to avoid getting into too complicated a plot which will be hard for the boys to follow or, worse yet, hard for you to follow.

(2) How to Tell the Story.

Tell it simply. Tell your story without flourish or attempt at great oratory. Keep it within the language range of the fellows to whom you are talking and use simple, clear sentences.

Tell it directly. Capture interest at the very start. Give no formal introductions. As soon as the last game is over, and without unnecessary preliminaries, start right in on the story. Pack action, interest, and enthusiasm into the first sentence.

Make your ending just as direct. Moralizing will spoil a story. Never finish a story and then add, "Now boys, 1 hope you all see that the point of this story is that we should always...etc." A good story delivers its own message and packs its own punch. This does not preclude a brief word applying the truth to the hearts of the fellows, but it should never be "preachy," nor should it be anything but very brief and right to the point.

Tell it dramatically. You should be able to visualize the story before you tell it. Then tell it as if you were actually in the story as one of the characters and were relating your own experiences. In other words, don't merely recite the story, live it. You will soon discover that your audience is not seeing or hearing you, but they are seeing and hearing the characters of a living story. They too, will be living with it.

(3) Story Sources.

The leader's story source is very wide. From the Bible he will obtain many stories both familiar and little known, which, when interpreted in terms of the experience of boys, will be his best One good method is to tell of events recorded in the Scriptures as they might have appeared to a boy of Brigade age living at the time. Sermon illustrations or stories found in Gospel tracts, adapted and dramatized, often make excellent Council Ring stories. Stories of pioneer missionaries from early church history right up to the present supply some of the best adventure tales possible. The Treasury furnishes further ideas along this line.

Leading Boys' Discussions

(1) The Planned Discussion

In preparing for a planned discussion the leader will first of all set down his objective. What is the point of the discussion, and what does he expect to accomplish through it?

The discussion topics may be obtained directly from the boys through a question box of some kind, or they may be chosen by the leader and announced some time before the discussion.

In the discussion itself the leader keeps things moving and guides the thinking of the group toward the objectives he wishes to accomplish. For instance, one topic may be "Does the Bible Teach Evolution?" In the discussion of the topic the leader will lead the discussion toward his objective of presenting the Bible account of creation to his group of high school boys.

This type of Council Ring gives the fellows a chance to take part and express their own ideas on the topics discussed. At the same time the Captain is accomplishing a planned purpose. The more thoroughly the leader is able to prepare on the topic the surer and more helpful he will be in the discussion.

(2) The Spontaneous Discussion

The best sort of discussion is the one which begins spontaneously with some fellow asking the question which in turn leads to other questions. The alert Captain will be ready (when the occasion fully warrants it) to lay aside his story or whatever else he has planned and follow through on such a spontaneous discussion. Before such a situation occurs, however, the Captain usually has come to know his boys rather well and understands their interests.

Again, the function of a discussion leader is to guide the direction of the discussion and to keep it moving along in interesting fashion. Recognize only one authority as final — the Word.

Usually the questions asked will be such as: "Why did God make man if He knew he was going to sin?" "Does the Bible say the earth is flat?" "Where did the Devil come from?" "Do animals have souls?" Especially among older boys, there'll be questions about science, evolution, and the "What's wrong with . . ." questions about amusements.

If you don't know the answer and can't turn to a Scripture on it, say so, but promise to look it up and tell them later. Then be sure to keep your promise. The bibliography in the Supplement will give you some suggestions on where to look for answers to questions on specialized subjects.

GIVING A STRAIGHT TALK TO BOYS

Used rightly and on the proper occasion, one of the best methods for making contacts with a group of fellows is just to talk right to them

Used wrongly or too often, it can ruin Council Ring time permanently for the fellows.

The Captain must have something definite and special to say. The straight talk in Council Ring should under no circumstances be considered the normal thing to be used. It is reserved for the time when the leader is particularly anxious to get certain truths across to the fellows, and believes, in light of his knowledge of the fellows and their confidence in him, that the best way to do it is to talk to them straight from the shoulder.

PRACTICAL PROBLEMS IN COUNCIL RING

(1) *How to handle wide age variation.* Within a Brigade Battalion, the age of fellows normally ranges from 12 to 18. Between those ages there is a certain difference in interests which presents problems to the leader preparing Council Ring for the group. A general rule that solves the problem is this. In *tone* and way of speaking aim at the oldest fellows present. (Avoid "talking down" to fellows, for boys appreciate having a man talk to them as men on his own level.) In choice of *words* and in simplicity of presentation, on the other hand, aim at the youngest boys present.

(2) *How to hold attention and keep order.* Council Ring is ruined and its effect practically erased when there is disorder among the fellows during the course of the leader's speaking. The leader who will tolerate slight disorder during Council Ring, will soon find that he has lost control completely. The following general principles will help in overcoming the problems. First, plan your Battalion program so that there are no delays or gaps. Nothing fosters disorder more quickly than an idle, boring time in the course of a meeting. Second, hold the fellows' interest. Don't expect attention if you aren't giving the boys anything worth listening to. Both what you say and how you say it should be interest holding.

CONCLUDING THE COUNCIL RING

It is seldom wise to delay the end of a meeting by any lengthy appeal, because boys become embarrassed by such and will be impatient to finish and be away. The Battalion meeting ends with the Council Ring and boys should always come to the end of a meeting wishing for more rather than wanting to get away. If they go home wishing for more, they'll be back the next week.

The evangelistic appeal or invitation following the story message is given differently to boys than it is given as a rule in an adult group. The main feature is brevity. If fellows know that there will not be a long appeal they are much more apt to respond at the very start. An invitation to stay and talk after the meeting is often fruitful and does not delay the meeting itself.

Under any circumstances in which a boy makes a public decision for Christ, follow it up with personal contact and prayer, both with him and for him.

Dismissal of the Battalion Meeting

Council Ring over, the Battalion meeting should be dismissed quickly. Rather than have any lengthy ceremony of dismissal, it works out better to let the fellows go home with the message of Council Ring still in their minds. Frequently the fellows stand together and sing the chorus or a verse and chorus of the Brigade Hymn, and then repeat to-gether the Brigade Watchword.

Normally, the Captain, Sergeant, and Corporals go into their brief "Non-com" meeting as soon as they are finished with any personal work opportunities that they may have following Council Ring.

The "Non-com" Meeting

For at least a few minutes after each Battalion meeting the Captain and perhaps his Lieutenants meet together with the non-commissioned officers — the Sergeant and Corporals — for a huddle on the progress of the Battalion. They discuss the meeting just completed, how they can make the next one better, mention special prayer requests, and discuss plans for future meetings.

This is another of the Captain's opportunities to train his junior leaders. At a time like this suggestions from the boys as to what games or other activities they like or do not like are discussed, and also sug-gestions from the Captain are given to the Corporals for better running of their Squad meetings or to the Sergeant for more effective follow-through on the Battalion meeting as a whole.

The key point of the "non-com" meeting, and an important spiritual link between the Captain and his junior leaders, is a period of united prayer which should always be included, even when there is time for nothing else.

BATTALION OUTDOOR ACTIVITY

Brigade, as a boy's program, would not be complete unless it included a liberal portion of outdoor activity. The largest single. phase of such activity will, of course, be summer camping. However, there are a variety of other outside activities, as for instance hiking, which can be used in the Battalion program throughout the year. The wise leader takes full advantage of his opportunities for getting outdoors with his gang.

Camping

WHY GO CAMPING?-

Camping is a magic word to the heart of a boy, for it represents adventure, accomplishment, and hearty fellowship. That, together with what tremendous things camping can do *for* a boy, place it high on the list of Brigade activity. This is true of the informal overnight trip, but is best applied to the official organized camp.

In the organized (more than overnight) camp, every aspect of a fellow's life is strengthened by the full round of camp activities and experiences.

Physical robustness and endurance are built up by plenty of vigorous exercise in a naturally healthful environment. Social strength is built by the normal give-and-take of the camp community's cooperative and competitive teamwork.

Spiritual understanding and growth come as the direct objective of the total camp program. In the camp frequent opportunities arise for Christian leaders to have personal and unhurried contact with individual boys. Here, too, it is possible to follow through a devotional and Bible study program which will provide fellows with needed spiritual food. And, as important as anything else, unsaved fellows can be won for Christ.

In the direct bearing upon the Battalion, Achievement progress, especially in the craft requirements, is a natural part of the camp program. All in all, the leader will find his gang returning from camp to the local Battalion with renewed interest, abilities, and zest.

INFORMAL CAMPING

High on the list of favorite Battalion activities are overnight outings, either by Squads or by the Battalion as a whole. Many groups who cannot get to an official camp will find this a second-best, but excellent substitute. Again, the secret of success is planning. Plot out the camping place, the route, the food, the equipment, and the activities — then get the gang together for a grand time!

ORGANIZED CAMP

The organized camp is one that is regularly set up and meets the standards of Brigade for a particular type of camp. It may be a Battalion, Frontier, Area, or Division camp. The organized camp is discussed here in brief to give the leader an over-all picture of this type of camp work. Complete details and standards are in the Brigade camp booklet, and can be had when needed by writing Brigade Headquarters.

(1) Camp Program

The following daily schedule is a standard sample of a Brigade camp day.

7:00 - Reveille, flag-raising, exercises, possibly morning dip.
7:30 - Morning lodge devotions.
8:00 - Breakfast, then camp clean-up.
9:15 - Inspection of quarters.
9:30 - Bible exploration hour.
10:15 - Morning craft period.
11:30 - Swim.
12:30 - Dinner.
1:30 - Rest period.
2:30 - Afternoon craft period.
3:30 - Afternoon planned activity; athletic contests, hikes, special activities of various sorts.
5:00 - Afternoon swim period.
6:00 - Supper, then free time.

7:30 - Flag-lowering.

7:45 - Campfire.

9:15 - Call to quarters, evening prayers.

9:30 - Taps.

As can be seen, the camp day has a full schedule. It is such a program, filled with well-paced, enjoyable activity, that makes time spent in camp fully worthwhile. Devotions, Bible study, crafts, athletics, campfires, and all the rest — each has a definite part in the schedule.

(2)   Kinds of Organized Camp

Bivouacs.   The little three to five-day bivouacs are "sample camps" which include all of the program features of Brigade camping in small doses.

Short Term Camps.   The one to two-week camps are long enough to allow the full Brigade camp program to get into fairly good swing. Craft certificates can be earned, and there is time to make definite headway in Bible exploration.

Long Term Camps.   Fully established long-term camps are run four, six, eight, or even ten weeks. They are often divided into two-week periods and these are so planned that each period is a program unit, yet the camp itself remains a continuous, well-varied camp unit.

Special activity camps and trips.   Well-organized and strongly-staffed leadership training camps; camps specializing in woodsmanship, marine activity, water safety, horsemanship, or aviation; and planned canoe trips, horseback trips, or cruises — all suggest a great variety of camping possibilities potentially available to older Brigadiers who have made considerable progress in their Achievement ranks and have thus qualified themselves for such activity.

(3)   Approved Brigade Camps

Four different types of Brigade camp have been authorized by the Brigade Board of Directors. Camps meeting the standards for any of these types and applying for approval to the Camp Committee of the Board of Directors, when approved are recognized as official Brigade camps and may use the Approved camp seal in their camp literature.

Battalion Camps.   Any camp under the sponsorship of a single Battalion or a group of individual Battalions, without any formal connection with Area or Division headquarters is termed a Battalion Camp. Battalion camps are governed by the Battalion Committee and Captain; or, in the case of joint Battalion sponsorship, by a camp committee consisting of the combined Battalion committees and Captains of the participating groups.

Frontier Camps. Frontier camps are pioneering camps used principally to introduce organized Brigade camping into new areas. The camp is operated on a joint basis. The business administration is handled by a local camp planning council and business manager recognized by the Camp Committee of the Board; program and personnel direction are undertaken by a Brigade Staff Officer, often aided by a service team of older Brigadiers trained to provide program leadership in camp. Request for a Frontier camp comes from the local camp planning council. Separation between Stockade-age and Battalion-age fellows is recommended, but method of division left to the discretion of the Camp Committee of the Board, the local camp planning council, and the camp director.

Area Camps. Area camps are those in operation in organized Brigade Areas under the jurisdiction of the Area Functional Committee. Stockaders and Brigadiers must be separated. The government of the Area camp is divided. Program and general direction are up to the camp director, who is the Staff Officer for the Area; business administration is handled by a camp committee set up by the Area Functional Committee.

Division Camps. Division camps may be operated by a Division headquarters for particular purposes within its territory or on a joint basis with another Division. The chief practical differences over the Area camp are the probability of extra program features, and the fact that Division camps are open only to Battalion-age Brigadiers. The responsibility for the direction of Division camps lies with a camp committee appointed by the Board of Directors.

Hiking

Hiking is closely related to camping. In the overnight camp, for instance, a large part of the program·is the hike to the camping spot.

Note carefully this basic fact about hiking: *A hike is more than a walk!* Hence, to be of any value to your Battalion program it must have both purpose and planning. Here are some suggested purposes: nature study, historic interest, definite exploration, quickened observation, appreciation of creation, physical fitness. The purpose chosen is not for announcement, but it is there for the leaders to follow through on. A good hike leader knows also the course of the hike, how far it's going to be, and the essential details from start to finish.

Some of the best hiking is done by Squads. Comradeship and teamwork are a top priority on hikes and the benefit to the Squad is large. Here also is an excellent way for further development of Corporal leadership.

One of the big features of hiking is that it is practically a year-round activity. As such, it can be tied in with a number of other events, as skating expeditions, swimming parties, wiener roasts. Further hike ideas will appear in the Treasury.

BATTALION ATHLETICS

For their appeal to boys and for what they do for them in physical strengthening and development of sportsmanship, athletic activities such as basketball, baseball, and the like rate a high place in the program. Never, however, let your sports program interfere with or supercede your regular weekly Battalion meeting. Brigade is not an athletic club and will not function long if used that way.

Developing athletic teams with an extra night a week for practice, possibly with a Lieutenant in charge, and getting into competition with other Battalions, provides a keen spur to increased Battalion interests.

BATTALION PROGRAM PLANNING

A successful Battalion program is the result of solid long-range and detailed planning. That does not imply hours of work. It does mean that the Battalion leaders have done some systematic thinking about the over-all work of their Battalion.

Long-range planning refers to laying out an outline of Battalion high spots, and it is usually convenient to plan on a year basis. Your high spots will include special activities and goals toward which to aim.

To begin long-range planning, get a schedule of the local area's yearly activities. That will form a good skeleton around which to build. Plan to take part in as much area activity as possible.

Next, take stock of your Battalion and decide on the goals for the year. Boys to be reached, Achievement progress, community and church projects, and similar factors — each should have a definite place in your year set-up.

Highlights of the individual months are next. It is well to plan on a quarterly seasonal basis (as provided in the Battalion Planning Chart). Within the season may be Rally month, Harvest month, Dad's month, Eskimo month, and the like. These titles will in turn be clues to the special activities and program to be developed.

Finally, there is your detailed planning where each month and then each week are considered. If your month's plans are clear, it will be simple to fit the weekly meetings into a systematic, yet varied pattern.

Planning your month's program with your non-coms will solve many potential problems of preparation and leadership. It's also excellent training for the non-coms and will give them added incentive for doing their best in the Battalion.

A planned Battalion program pays. It will provide you with goals to work toward. You can point toward the special activities and build them up. It will keep you out of ruts of program and activity. Above all, it will give you as a leader confidence in the work, and give your Battalion a coordinated, livewire program.

THE STOCKADE IN ACTION

There are many general principles involved in the Battalion meeting that apply also to the Stockade. However, a different type of meeting is planned for the Stockader. There are two main reasons for this. First, the Stockade meeting has been laid out for the 8-11 age boy with his particular characteristics and interests in mind (as given in the first chapter). It is a type of meeting definitely planned for his age. The Stockade is not a "junior Battalion."

Second, the Stockade meeting is kept distinct from the Battalion meeting as another factor in keeping the interest of the boys. Thus, the boy who goes from the Stockade into the Battalion will find an entirely new program of activities. The Battalion meeting will be new and fresh to him.

It is of great importance, therefore, to keep the units separate for the success of both the Stockade and the Battalion in the local church. When they are combined the harm is more immediately noticeable in the Battalion, but the Stockade program will also suffer considerably. The best situation is usually for the Stockade and Battalion to meet on separate nights. Where it is necessary to have them on the same evening, use available meeting space in such a way that the groups do not interfere with each other.

Stockade Posts

The Stockade is divided into smaller groups called Posts, made up of from 4 to 10 boys. A full Stockade has four Posts (North, East, South, West). Each Post is led by an adult leader called Ranger (or "Guide," if not yet qualified as Ranger).

The Posts are divided as evenly as possible, so that competition between Posts is on a fair basis. A Post should hardly ever have more than ten boys. When a Stockade begins to average more than 40 boys, consideration should be given to dividing into another Stockade group. Each Post should have a balance of Builder and Sentinel age boys. Although there is an Achievement separation for the 8-9 and 10-11 ages, this is not a meeting program separation, and it is important that the meeting program be for all Stockaders together.

Normally, the Sentinel age boys stand on the right and Builder age boys on the left. However, if there is a considerable difference in the proportion of Builders to Sentinels, the sides can be evened out.

There are two honor positions for each Post: *Lookout* (10-11 years old), and *Courier* (8-9 years old). Refer to the LOG, pp. 7-11 for a review of their duties and formation positions. As indicated in the LOG, these positions are rotated among the Stockaders. A Duty List is kept and boys become eligible for these positions when they are actively working on Achievement; changes generally occur each month. A boy's name may be passed over in this list for misbehaviour, but this should not be done without ample warning and only when the misbehaviour is persistent.

Stockade Council Meeting

The weekly Stockade meeting is called the Stockade Council. Afternoon Councils may work out well, but in general the evening seems preferable, with emphasis on an early and promptly dismissed meeting.

A TYPICAL STOCKADE COUNCIL PROGRAM

7:00 - "Build the Stockade" — Chief Ranger in Charge.
  (1) "Build the Stockade" — Rangers, Lookouts, Couriers, Stockaders.
  (2) "Stockade Silence" — prayer.
  (3) "Count Stockaders" — attendance.
  (4) "Colors — Salute — Banners" — flag ceremony.
7:10 - Stockade Games and Contests — Rangers in charge.
7:30 - Post Meetings (Post business and Sparker activity) — Rangers in charge.
8:00 - Stockade Honors — Chief Ranger in charge.
8:10 - Stockade Story Time — Rangers or visitor.
8:25 - Dismiss — Stockade Benediction.

(Review carefully the STOCKADE COUNCIL section in the LOG, pp. 8-11).

A. *"Build the Stockade"*. This call is given by the Chief Ranger as the signal for the opening of the Stockade meeting. Everyone is expected to stop his activity immediately and quietly face the center of the room. Do not give further calls until there is complete attention.

Rangers (or Guides) take their positions in the Block formation. Then the Lookouts and Couriers move to their places. Finally the Stockaders fill in the formation. When the Stockade is well established, this formation should be almost one movement. If necessary at first, the Chief Ranger can help by actually calling out *"Rangers," "Lookouts and Couriers,"* and *"Stockaders"* in order, allowing time for each group to get to their positions.

The key to success in forming the Stockade this way lies in the leaders themselves knowing the formations, for they lead the others. Especially when just starting the Stockade it is well to have the leaders practice this opening formation at the meeting place before meetings are actually held with the boys. The exact positions may be marked on the floor of the meeting place if this is possible.

It will help in the Stockade formation for both leaders and the boys to keep in mind the picture of an actual stockade — the Posts at each corner and the walls (Stockaders) are on each side of the square.

Immediately after the Stockade has been formed, the Chief Ranger gives the call, "Stockade, *silence.*" This prepares the group for prayer, and after the prayer, for introduction of visitors and other announcements.

"Count Stockaders," is the signal for the attendance check to be taken. This is done by one of the Rangers standing by the Stockade Roster (record board that has a Notch-stick for each Stockader) and reporting the attendance of each Post. Each Notch-stick should be in its proper place, put there by the Stockader himself when he arrives at the meeting. For further information on the Stockade Roster and Notch-sticks, refer to the Roster information included with organizing materials.

The presenting of colors is accomplished by three calls from the Ranger. At *"Colors"* the Ranger of the Honor Post carries the national flag and the Lookout of the Honor Post carries the Stockade flag to the center of the formation. When the call, *"Salute,"* is given, each Courier dips his Post banner straight forward while all pledge allegiance to the national flag. At the call *"Banners,"* the flags and the Post banners are set back in their places.

B. *Stockade Games and Contests.* There are two types of games in the Stockade, listed simply as Type A and Type B. The "A" games are the more active games and are to be played first in the meeting. The "B" games have more restricted action and are planned to give the leader a type of situation where he can move easily into the next activity, the Post meetings.

The games that are best suited for Stockaders are those that involve individual competition rather than teamwork. Avoid using Battalion games for the Stockade — your Stockaders will want to play them later as Battalion members. Never waste time in getting started with the game time, nor in changing from game to game. Each new game must be explained carefully and it should be played just as explained. Refer to pp. 79-86 of this manual for additional game leadership suggestions.

If the boys are lined up by Posts at the close of the game time, they can be dismissed directly to Post meetings. Otherwise, the Chief Ranger gives the command, *"Build the Stockade,"* and the boys are dismissed by Posts to Post meetings.

C. *Post Meetings.* This is the Achievement time in the Stockade, and is led by the Post Ranger. Builder and Sentinel Achievement work is completed and checked during this time. During Post meetings all available adult leadership is needed to keep all boys occupied and to help individual boys as much as possible.

At the opening of the Post meeting, matters of Post business are quickly taken care of — such things as Post plans (perhaps a hike or special group project), announcements, and collecting shares. Shares are the boys' contributions toward the expenses of the group. Shares at the first meeting of the month are designated as "missionary shares" and given for missionary work, either through Brigade Headquarters or through the local church.

The main part of the Post meeting is the "Stockade Sparker" activity. The Sparker may be a project or tool demonstration by one of the Rangers; it may consist of time spent on a particular Handyman project by the boys themselves. Sparker activities are usually on an individual Post basis, but occasionally two Posts or the whole Stockade may join together (e.g., for an educational film showing).

Post Rangers can often specialize in a certain project and then exchange Posts to lead the project for several meetings. However, the Ranger should be with his Post for the rest of the meeting, leaving only to lead another Post in the project.

To assist in Achievement test checking, Rangers may sometimes "double up" with one Ranger supervising a project for two Posts while the other Ranger works with boys on passing tests. This may allow more personal time with boys, especially on opportunities to deal with them concerning spiritual matters. If there is sufficient adult leadership, it is well for the Chief Ranger to be free of Post responsibility in order to be available for test checking during the entire Post meeting time.

Although this is not the age of strong team spirit, the leader should

(This section continued in the Appendix at the back, p. 129)

CHAPTER OUTLINE

A SURVEY OF THE CAPTAIN'S WORK

Leading your Battalion
Working with your Church
Working with your Battalion Committee
Working together with your Lieutenants
Training your Non-coms
Filling a position in your Community

THE CAPTAIN GUIDING BOYS

Occasions for Guidance
Leading a Boy to Christ
The Gospel in the Brigade Achievement Program

TRAINING A BOY FOR CHRIST

Spiritual Growth
Counsel in Personal Problems
Leadership
Discipline
Looking Ahead

CHAPTER SEVEN

Captain in Action

A SURVEY OF THE CAPTAIN'S WORK

Leading your Battalion

Most of your activity as a Captain will, of course, center around the Battalion. So let's just take a typical Battalion night and follow some of the action.

You're away from the supper table a little early this particular night in order to get to your Battalion meeting in plenty of time. Down at the meeting place you meet the Sergeant and Corporals also getting there early, and together with them and your Lieutenants, you run through the meeting plans and give the program the final "once over". Each leader knows his part, and you're ready to run the meeting as a team.

Now, as the other fellows arrive, you greet them by name, but you are particularly interested in getting to know new fellows that may be out tonight. The Sergeant and other non-coms have started informal games to fill the interval before the meeting begins.

At the dot of seven-thirty, if that is your appointed time, you instruct the Sergeant to call for the Battalion line-up. As the Corporals and Sergeant order the Squads into line, you are waiting, ready for when the Sergeant reports, "The Battalion is formed, Sir." Then you commit the evening to the Lord in prayer.

Your own activity throughout the Battalion meeting follows the pattern of these first minutes. You are not supposed to "run" the Battalion, but rather to guide it. The very make-up of the Battalion itself involves action, and your job is to steer that action.

A lot depends upon your enthusiasm. Fellows look to you as their leader and your own fervor is the spark that ignites their fervor. Consecrated enthusiasm is a tremendously potent force. It can hurdle seemingly impossible obstacles and carry a gang through to unity and loyalty. A hike over a mountain or forest trail can be an exciting adventure filled with long-remembered thrilling experiences, or on the other hand it can became a dull and tiresome exertion. The difference depends upon one factor, namely the enthusiasm or lack of it on the part of the leader One leader starts off without much pep and before he has gone six steps some boy will ask, "Do I have to go?" Another leader shouts, "O boy! Let's get going. I want to see what's beyond that ridge!" And the fellows come home dead tired, but telling of the wonderful hike they had.

Enthusiasm is highly contagious. If properly exposed to it, older boys of leadership caliber are nearly certain to contract it, and they prove excellent carriers.

Working with your church

As leader of your Battalion, which is an integral part of the church program, you are a leader in the church.

With your Committee and pastor, you will want to carefully co-ordinate all Battalion activities with the total program of the church. You will also be keeping alert for opportunities whereby the Battalion can be of definite service in the church. Every activity is worthwhile which will give the boys a keener appreciation of the church or which will give the people of the church a better understanding of Brigade and the aims of the Battalion.

Working with your Battalion Committee

As Captain you are a member of the Committee ex-officio, as is also your pastor. You will want to meet regularly as a Committee — at least once every two months. But in addition you will be in frequent contact with them, possibly during occasional short meetings after church to consider certain business that may come up concerning the Battalion.

Here are two good rules for successful work with your Committeemen:

1. *Know them.* Become well acquainted with each one of your Committeemen both as a friend and as co-worker. Know the abilities and interests of each one, and thus their potentialities for special help in the Battalion program. Become acquainted with their strength as

individuals and know something of the contacts they may have that will be of value to the work.

2. *Counsel with them.* Come to them for help, for guidance in important decisions, and for the sharing of inspiration in the work. The Captain is responsible to the Committee, not the Committee to the Captain. Have them attend Battalion meetings whenever possible to get the feel of the work. Remember, however, that they are primarily Committeemen If they wish to help with the actual leadership of the meetings, use them, but appoint them Lieutenants for that part of their relationship to Brigade.

Together with your Committee you will plan the long-range program of your Battalion, set up the aims and objectives, and plan the activity channels 'which will lead to their realization. More important than any other single aspect of your counseling together with your Committeemen will be your time spent with them in prayer. Praying together as men for your boys and for the guidance of the Lord in laying and carrying out your plans will do more than any other thing to bring about real spiritual unity among you, which spiritually will most surely be reflected in the nature of the Battalion.

Working together with your Lieutenants

Only commissioned officers (Captains and Lieutenants) are author ized to officially approve boys for advancement in Brigade Achievement tests. Eighteen-year-old First Lieutenants and sixteen-year-old Second Lieutenants' are commissioned only because they have fully and clearly shown that they have the qualifications necessary for a Brigade officer.

The primary responsibility of the Lieutenant is to work personally with boys. He is an extension of the Captain. Your non-coms — Sergeant and Corporals — have leadership responsibility, to be sure, but their jobs are clearly defined and laid out for them.

The Lieutenant, on the other hand, is an officer, a man capable of taking a man's leadership. That means he does not need to have his personal activity outlined for him. During Squad meetings the Lieutenant is available to pass boys on their Achievement tests. Here he is thrown into individual personal contact with the fellows. During the remainder of the meeting he shares the leadership of Battalion activity with his Captain as planned before the meeting began.

The Lieutenant's leadership during the week between regular Battalion meetings is very important.   One Lieutenant in a large Battalion might be in charge of athletic activities, another might lead the outings, still another might guide during-the-week craft clubs for woodworking, radio, or other such shop crafts.   No one man can be well versed in all of the activities that you will eventually want to include in your Battalion program, but through your Lieutenants you can effect a widely talented leadership for your Battalion.

Second Lieutenants, fellows sixteen and seventeen who are commissioned as officers, are rare.   The rank exists, however, for the encouragement of young fellows who have proved themselves in junior leadership positions and through their Achievement in Brigade, and are ready to take mature leadership responsibility to do the equivalent of a man's job.

Training your Non-coms

Non-commissioned officers in the Battalion are the Sergeant, who is in charge of all line-ups and keeps the meeting moving according to schedule; the Corporals, normally four, leading the Squads; and the Lance-Corporals assisting the Corporals.   Together, they represent one of the greatest training potentialities of your Battalion.   A most important aspect of your job as Captain is the guidance and development of these junior leaders.

Battalion non-coms range in age from about fourteen to eighteen. The typical Corporal is sixteen, the typical Sergeant, seventeen.   They are at an age when their leadership possibilities are high; yet they are immature and uncertain of themselves, and therefore generally very willing to be given guidance in regard to leading other fellows.

The boys of your gang whom you choose as being of leadership caliber are naturally the "cream" of the outfit.   Normally these fellows have more influence on other boys in the community than anyone else and are in closer contact with them.   That means that if these junior leaders are once thoroughly sold on Brigade and have entered into it whole-heartedly, then you as a Captain working through them have an ideal opportunity to reach the unreached fellows of the community.

At the end of each Battalion meeting you have a short "Non-com huddle" with your junior leaders for prayer and discussion of both the meeting just over and one for the following week. Here will be your opportunity as a Captain to give helpful guidance to those fellows in leadership development.

As you pray for your non-coms and seek to train them, it is well to recognize three basic needs of young fellows starting out in service for Christ.

They need spiritual guidance. Being young Christians, they do not have the backlog of experience that older Christian workers have to guide them in plotting their course. By the very fact that they are undertaking service for Christ, they will have spiritual battles to fight. Temptations will be stronger. As they are giving out to other fellows, their own need for taking in spiritual food will be the greater. Take every opportunity to talk with them individually and together about spiritual truths. Explain the Word to them and pray with them often.

They need fellowship with older leaders. As they share leadership responsibilities with commissioned officers in the Battalion, the young fellows get the feel of more mature responsibility. They learn to "think leadership." Plan occasions such as hikes, suppers retreats where leadership fellowship can be fostered.

They need exercise in leadership by actually taking responsibility. As they prove themselves in little things, they must be given opportunity to prove themselves in more important things. To develop leadership, a boy must have leadership opportunity.

Filling a position in your community

As associated with boys, you will be considered as their friend by the boys and by their parents and by other adults of the community.

Your own Battalion boys will of course, come to you, as they get to know you, for advice in many things. But even other fellows in the community may find their way to you because of your interest in boys.

Likewise, many fathers and mothers, faced with problems that concern their sons, are desperate for the counsel of a man who is able to give them sound advice.

In addition to guidance opportunities, your relation to your community is effected greatly by opportunities for you and your Battalion to be of direct service. In community emergencies you can be of great service as a Battalion, being a group of boys already organized for action under the leadership of able men. Messengers, watchmen, directors of traffic, and other helpers can be provided by the Battalion when needed. When a community realizes that its Christian Service Brigade Battalion is ready and able to go into action on projects such as these, the Battalion represents a powerful testimony for Christ to that community.

Besides definite projects of service, there are also such ways as parades and patriotic festivals in which you and your Battalion can enter into community life.

There are several individuals in the community whom either you or your Committeemen would do well to know. The superintendents or principals of the high schools and grade schools that your boys attend, as well as the truant officers, are good contacts. Frequently these men will gladly contact you in cases where there are boys who need your help, and they will nearly always appreciate your interest in fellows that may be presenting problems to them.

In small towns or cities a Captain should be acquainted with the police chief. In a metropolis, he may value a contact with the judge of the juvenile court. Though your boys may never have any contact with these men, you will have opportunity to learn a lot about what goes on when a boy gets on the wrong track, and you may have opportunity to rescue fellows from the sort of life to which a boyhood criminal record usually leads.

THE CAPTAIN GUIDING BOYS

It's one thing to have a tool; it's quite another thing to use it. That's why this section is among the most important in the manual, for we discuss here how the Captain uses the Brigade program in meeting the need of boys.

The entire Brigade program is set up to provide channels for winning and training boys. How those channels are used depends upon the Captain. What he does and says, for instance, when a boy comes to him to pass a certain Achievement test may determine whether that fellow is led to Christ or not. This chapter on guidance — making full use of the program with a definite purpose in mind -— aims to equip the Captain for making the most of his many guidance opportunities.

In that the program is geared to provide personal contact, his guidance opportunities will be constant and natural. Of course, the Captain is guiding by his own life and guiding also the group as a whole, but the richest and most focal times are those of direct, personal counsel. In the Achievement tests, on hikes, in camp — the boy and his leader are on talking ground.

What an opportunity is yours, Captain, for seeing fellows become new creatures in Christ, watching them become strong in the Lord, as you take advantage of these opportunities!

One further introductory word about guidance. Brigade is concerned with every sphere of a boy's life. ". . . for Christ" touches every aspect of living. Hence, there are included in this guidance section — besides the primary factors of salvation and spiritual growth — personal problems, discipline, leadership, and vocations.

Occasions for Guidance

Place. Your principle place of meeting with fellows will, of course, be at the Battalion meeting itself. Coming together here from week to week should soon give your fellows the feeling that this is a place where they can come with problems and find counsel and help. Church building and the Sunday School rooms often furnish other places where the leader has opportunity to chat with a boy that may need his help.

Hikes and outings of various sorts are good occasions for personal talks. And camp, of course, affords perhaps the most outstanding opportunities for effective counsel work.

Besides these more common places, there are others that can often be used. Gym locker rooms, street corners, homes — all may become counsel ground.

Time. Almost without exception, your best time for guidance is the time *when a boy comes to you* or in some way is in the position of seeking help. And here lies the great significance of the Achievement program in Brigade, for it provides in a natural way this sort of contact between man and boy, Captain and Brigadier.

Bob was a thirteen-year-old freckled farm boy who met once each week in the country school house with other fellows in the community—there were about ten in all — for their Brigade Battalion meeting. What excitement there was when the new Brigade guidebooks were handed out (the first edition) with thrilling things to do and to learn.

Although the program then was only a shadow of its present set-up, those boys in the country school house hit into the advancement tests in earnest. Soon Bob was ready to pass his Brigade pledge.

"Trusting in the Lord Jesus Christ," he recited slowly when time came for recitation, "and in Him alone as my Saviour..." The leader and he talked about what it meant. Bob had some questions, and when he felt quite sure that he understood what trusting the Lord Jesus meant, he decided right then and there that he wanted to put his trust in Him.

"Are you sure you are trusting in Him alone?" his Captain asked.

Bob opened his blue eyes wide and looked right square into the leader's — "Why, there isn't anybody else!" Right then they knelt down beside the wooden school benches and Bob gave his heart to the Lord Jesus Christ.

Bob was the first boy to earn a Brigade Achievement rank. Of course, his becoming a Christian was not part of the rank, and Bob well realized it. But, note again, his coming to pass that very first test was the occasion which led directly to Bob's coming to Christ. Ever since that initial experience, boys all across the land, coming to their Captains to report steps forward in their Achievement progress, have learned, through that friendly contact with their Captains, to know Christ as their Savior.

Opportunity. Opportunities for guidance come up naturally from time to time. It is important to recognize them in order to be able to take advantage of them in helping your fellows.

THE TIME WHEN A BOY COMES TO YOU WITH A QUESTION, or when questions come up naturally in normal conversation, may be the manifestation of a felt need on his part. Don't be mysterious and act as if you were psychoanalyzing a boy, but on the other hand, the question he asks may not be the question he really wants to ask. The man who works with boys soon learns to evaluate and understand boys' questions and interprets the thing a boy means not only by what he says but also by the way he says it.

WHEN A BOY COMES WITH A REQUEST — to be passed in an Achievement test, to be instructed in some skill, or to be given some particular responsibility — or when in any way he is in the position of wanting something from you, an opportunity for guidance is presented.

WHEN A BOY REALIZES HIS SPIRITUAL NEED, the greatest of counseling opportunities is open to you. At the end of Council Ring or after campfire time in camp, you may give an invitation for any boy who wants to make sure about his relationship to Christ to stay around and talk and pray about it. This sort of invitation leaves the initiative to the boy but opens the way for him to come. Counsel at such a time in helping a boy to find Christ or to settle problems in his Christian life counts for most because it is meeting a boy at the time when he realizes his need and presenting to him the Christ who is able to completely meet that need.

DOING A JOB TOGETHER WITH A BOY provides a singularly opportune contact for counseling and direct guiding — also a good chance to see a side of a boy not always easy to see. Ed, by way of actual illustration, was a fellow whom his Captain found hard to get to know. Then came a time when the Battalion went out for an overnight hike. The Captain and Ed drew the job of getting supper ready while the other fellows played a lively game of "Pioneers and Indians." By the time the wood was gathered and the fire built up and blazing away under the "Mulligan Stew," Ed had begun to feel the warm comradeship that comes from fellow workmen on a job. It was only natural then, as the two sat down to rest, for them to start talking about serious things, including Ed's relation to Christ. Before that chat was finished, Ed had taken a stand for Christ. Today he is active in his Battalion, growing in the Lord and increasing in leadership.

WHEN A BOY IS ENTERING UPON SOMETHING NEW AND BIG — a crisis time in his life—he is at a place in his maturing when guidance is much needed, and usually much wanted, if rightly given. This is very true in the spiritual sense for a boy who has accepted Chrst as his Saviour and is entering upon the new adventure of living for Him: he is in the greatest need of spiritual guidance. In the face of other crises, too, real opportunity and occasion for guidance are offered. An older fellow who has been growing up through the stages of Brigade Achievement may suddenly come to the point where he leaves the gang to enter into military service or go away to college. At times such as this a fellow in Brigade should think naturally of his Captain as the person he wants to go to for counsel and advice.

Times of crises in a boy's life are not necessarily as evident to others as they are to him. Things that seem of minor importance to you may loom large to the point of view of the fellow himself — graduation from grade school, a first job, a first date, a first time away to camp, and many other "firsts" are actually of great significance in the life of a boy, and how he is guided in each of these things has its lasting effect on his life.

Leading a boy to Christ

This work for which Brigade primarily exists — the work of winning boys for Christ — is not the work of man but the work of the Holy Spirit. Our procedure, accordingly, cannot be like the ordinary "how to do" discussion, laying out angles of approach and systems of technique. It is rather seeking, through the Word of God, to understand the way in which the Holy Spirit works to convict boys of sin and draws them to Christ, and of our place and responsibility as leaders of boys in *leading* them to Him.

1. THE HOLY SPIRIT'S WORK

The Holy Spirit is the agent in accomplishing the new birth. (Read again the third chapter of John, the first eight verses; read also the sixteenth chapter, verses seven to fifteen.) When a boy comes to Christ he is *born of the Spirit*, who bears witness of the fact that he is a child of God.

There are three important facts to be noted concerning the way in which the Holy Spirit works. They are these: (a) He works through the Word of God (Romans 10:17). (b) He works as men pray (Acts 4:31-33). He works through faithful personal witness (Romans 10:13-14).

The Word of God presents fully the message of salvation. Leading a boy to Christ requires constant dependance upon the Word — in quoting and in actually showing the boy the verses in the Bible. If the boy's trust is in the written Word he has a solid foundation.

Prayer is a means God has provided for making available His power
The leader of boys who will be fruitful is one who is close enough to his
Lord and burdened of heart enough to pray effectively for the salvation
and strengthening of his boys.

Personal witness, the telling of the Gospel, is the means which God
uses for His Word to be implanted in boys' hearts. Our part as witnesses
is to proclaim to boys fully the Lord Jesus Christ.

2. PRESENTING THE GOSPEL

The presentation of the Gospel is a serious matter. Although a
person may often be very clear as to the application of salvation to his own
life, the explanation of it to someone else may be confused and even
misleading. The suggestions given here are aimed to give the Captain
a practical foundation in presenting the Gospel to his boys.

a. KEEP THE MESSAGE SIMPLE AND CLEAR.

Unless the claims of Christ are presented simply and plainly in a
way that the boy can clearly understand — described in terms of things
that the boy himself knows — there is danger that he may become confused and lose sight of the great important guide-posts, namely, recognition of himself as a sinner and Christ as the Saviour who can cleanse him
from his sin.

It is possible for a boy to make a lip profession while his heart is
still far from Christ. This is especially apt to happen if the issue is
blurred and the message presented in a way which is not clear and direct.
Social pressure may lead a boy to go ahead and give the right answers
without worrying about what they mean.

In making the message clear, one important thing to watch is the
use of words that are commonly used and perfectly understood among
Christians but which may mean nothing or something altogether different to boys who have no Christian background. An outstanding
example: One after another of the fellows around a certain campfire
circle were standing to testify that they were saved by the Lord Jesus.
Jimmy, a little fellow, listened for quite a time, then decided he wanted
to be in on it too. "I'm glad God saved me," he said. "When I was
little, I ran out into the street once when there was a big truck coming and
it almost hit me, but God saved me." He sat down.

His leader talking with him later, found that Jimmy had no idea at all of the meaning of salvation or what it meant to be saved from sin, yet in the sense in which the boy understood it, God had indeed saved him from being killed by the truck. There was nothing wrong with the term "saved," but its meaning as used at the campfire needed to be made clear.

b. TELL THE WHOLE MESSAGE.

That is, include all the facts that are needed to present the simple Gospel message completely. There are several essentials that must be noted if a complete picture is to be given. When talking to a boy about accepting Christ, be sure he understands these three things: (1) *his own need*, (2) *what the Lord has done to meet his need*, (3) *how he can take advantage of the way God has met his need.*

(1) *Make sure the boy knows his own need.* Salvation means little without an initial realization of something to be saved from. One cannot win a boy to Christ without talking about the boy's sin and consequent need for a Saviour.

The natural consciousness of sin can be emphasized through Scripture verses such as Romans 3:23 and Isaiah 53:6. It is often helpful also to explain the origin of sin, as given in Genesis 3. Finally, to give point to the presentation of sin, the penalty for it must be shown from verses like Ezekiel 18:20 and Romans 6:23.

In this way, by careful and illustrated explanations, the boy will see his need for salvation, based on his sinful nature, his sins, and the consequence of this condition in the light of God's holiness.

(2) *Show what the Lord has done to meet the boy's need.* God in His love for the sinner gave His Son Jesus Christ to die for our sins. Romans 5:8 and I John 4:10 are excellent for use here. Point out that the person can do nothing himself for his sins, but salvation is entirely of the Lord. Verses like Ephesians 2:8,9 and Acts 4:12, will demonstrate this clearly and in turn will emphasize the great, overwhelming love of God that sent Christ to Calvary. Boys can understand this substitutionary work of Christ for them when verses such as I Peter 3:18 and 2:24 and the conclusion of Isaiah 53:6 are explained and illustrated to them.

(3) *Explain how the boy can take advantage of the way God has met his need.* The boy personally takes Christ as *his* Saviour. This appeal to action is the way to make all else you say about salvation bear fruit. Receiving the Lord Jesus can be graphically portrayed to boys by pressing home the meaning of John 1:10-12. John 3:16 or 20:31 and verses such as Romans 10:9,10 and Acts 16:31 picture, too, the way of this acceptance. Notice the clear way in which "belief" is set forth by Mr. J. F. Strombeck in his article for boys in the BOY'S GUIDE-BOOK, p. 48.

In praying with a boy when he says he is ready to make his decision, take time to allow him to phrase his thoughts in his own words. Don't urge or press, but in every way possible make the boy feel your own thoughtful reverence as you pray with him.

c. FOLLOW THROUGH ON DECISIONS

Follow through with fellows after they have come to know Christ as Saviour. One of the biggest struggles in a boy's spiritual life normally comes right after he has taken Christ as his own Saviour. Then is when the enemy of souls wages his biggest warfare. There are two primary methods of Satan. He either tries to intimidate through some other person — unsaved parents, or scoffing chums; or he seeks to turn the new believer into other channels of thinking, through doubts as to what God has done for him, and through the renewed influence of worldly habits and acquaintances.

In combating these temptations, the leader can help his boys best by two means. First, show again what took place when the boy came to know Christ (as explained in John 3:3; II Corinthians 5:17; Romans 5:8). Second, urge him to begin and maintain his three essentials for a healthy Christian life — Bible reading, prayer, and witnessing for the Lord.

3. THE GOSPEL IN THE BRIGADE ACHIEVEMENT PROGRAM

It has been noted before how certain Brigade Achievement tests act as a springboard for talks with boys about salvation. The program as a whole is designed for the purpose of drawing boys to Christ. However, there are these certain parts of the program which present the Gospel

directly and are the leader's particular opportunity for winning individual boys to Christ.

The Explorer's Verses — John 1:10-12 — form one of the very
best portions of Scripture to put before a fellow in helping him to know
the truths about salvation. These verses declare the issue clearly between those who are rejectors and those who are receivers of the Lord
Jesus. The father-son relationship is within the boy's understanding and
helps him grasp the meaning of salvation.

The Seven Points of Valor are included in both the Explorer and
Trailblazer ranks. Explaining them gives good opportunity to apply
the Gospel message, especially in the case of Purity, Obedience, and
Consecration. For example, a fellow cannot be really pure unless he
is cleansed from sin through the blood of Christ.

The Brigade Pledge, together with the Scripture on which it is
built, has been the means of contact through which many boys in Brigade
have come to know Christ as their Saviour. One of its purposes is to
make certain that every boy advancing through Brigade understands the
way of salvation. Any explanation of it must include God's plan of
redemption as a necessary part of the explanation. Again the leader
is given the chance to find out where a boy stands in regard to his Christian profession.

All of the Scripture verses included as memory work in the Achievement tests, as well as the Scripture required to be read, present the Gospel
of Christ to boys. When a boy comes to his leader to recite a verse he
has memorized, the leader has opportunity to check his understanding
of the verse. And when he comes to report a Scripture reading portion
completed, the natural question is, "What did it say?" giving the boy
a chance to give it in his own words. If the boy is hazy on Bible meaning, the leader can get into the Word with him and help him to have a
deeper appreciation of its message.

*   *   *   *   *   *   *

In all of your contact with those boys of yours, remember above
everything else that the source of power whereby a boy can be won for
Christ is the Holy Spirit Himself. Don't expect Brigade Achievement or
any other phase of the program to have saving power.

Let God guide you, too, as you talk with boys, in how much to say. Guard constantly against bringing a boy to a lip confession of Christ made in order to please you. Often the pressure of some special meeting or some emotional crisis may cause a boy to make a big profession without having thought through what he means by it. Genuine conviction of the Holy Spirit and a sincere heart decision are the soul-winner's two guide-posts.

The joy of leading boys to Christ lies before you, Captain!

TRAINING A BOY FOR CHRIST

What about the Christian boys in your Battalion? They should be growing as well-rounded Christian fellows. Again, the Brigade program gives you channels through which to train them in this growth. Both by individual counsel and group instruction the Captain has opportunity to guide boys in becoming "Bright and Keen for Christ."

General occasions for guidance have already been discussed under a previous section. As in leading a boy to Christ, these can be applied specifically in training the boy through the Achievement program. Hence, the leader should be well acquainted with the Achievement program, understand its implication in the life of the boy, and have in mind his place in using and interpreting it for the boy.

Even more so than in leading a boy to Christ, the training phase requires the leader's help. The program itself cannot answer the boy's many questions or adapt its training for the individual need. That is the Captain's opportunity and responsibility.

Spiritual Growth

In some cases circumstances may be such that your Battalion meeting will be the only source of spiritual food for certain fellows. What you provide in the way of spiritual menu will determine their Christian growth. On the other hand, the fellows should be encouraged to maximum church activity. Brigade is not a boy's church; it is a phase of the church's work.

In helping the boy grow in Christ during your Battalion contact, keep in mind the three basic factors of *prayer, Bible study,* and *consecration.*

Use prayer in your meetings, talk about prayer, and pray individually with the fellows. Help them become real prayer warriors.

The Scriptures are of paramount importance — your boys must be taught to read and study them if their Christian life is to count. Make the Word the center of their spiritual thinking.

Consecration involves living, serving, and witnessing. It means honoring the Lord in everything. Under this will come questionable amusements, school testimony, church work, full-time Christian work, and a number of similar topics.

To live for Christ is a challenge — a challenge, as Paul wrote to Timothy, "to be a good soldier of Jesus Christ." Never give a fellow the idea that to be a Christian is a "cinch." He'll know better after a few of Satan's temptations and discouragements. One of the biggest things you can do for that young Christian fellow is to arm him well for the Christian fight with the weapons of prayer, the Word, and a consecrated life.

Counsel in Personal Problems

Nearly every fellow longs for the sort of friend who is a man in years and experience, and yet is able to understand the sort of problems that face boys. In being such a friend, pray earnestly for your boys. Time spent in talking to God about a boy is a necessary companion to time spent in talking to a boy about God.

Here are some general thoughts on talking with boys about personal problems in their lives. First, be careful not to exaggerate a problem. Sometimes a leader seeking to help a fellow will by sheer weight of talk make his problem appear entirely out of proportion. This will serve to discourage a fellow rather than to help him.

Then, above all, be friendly. Avoid being professional or talking like an expert on boy problems. Usually a fellow doesn't really want the advice half as much as the friendship and steadying encouragement that the leader can give and which in turn will help the boy meet the issue at hand himself.

The problems are many and widely varied which face a boy as he goes through the process of growing up, and to cover or even refer to them all here is impossible. But there are a few typical problems that do come up frequently in boys' lives which a leader ought to understand. Such problems include spiritual life, home, school, work, and sex.

Discipline

Discipline — the part of boys' work which presents the greatest problems to some leaders and even causes some to fail—is a part of guidance. Regarded as such and as a very positive thing, it should not present an insurmountable problem to the boys' leader. By definition — *discipline* is not synonymous with punishment — it involves far more. It means training, sometimes strict, always firm, and in our case, kind.

GROUP CONTROL

The first question facing the Captain in discipline problems is the matter of keeping order in the gang. There is no excuse for a poorly disciplined Christian boys' club group. Boys have little respect for a leader who cannot keep order and they do not enjoy activities in which discipline is lacking. This fact is true, even though the very boys who feel that way about it may contribute to the disorder themselves. The objectives of the program are hindered, perhaps defeated, in a meeting which is disorderly. By definition, a disorderly meeting is essentially lack of cooperation. This may consist of direct disobedience to rules, principles, or individuals.

There are basically three reasons for disorder among boys. Of these three, the first two are much harder to overcome, but the third is responsible for a major part of the trouble boys' leaders face.

Some boys are disorderly because they want to be. They have definite objectives in their misbehavior — they want to oppose the purposes of the leader and keep the club from succeeding. Be careful, however, in putting boys into this class, for they are few and far between. The boys who are really opposed usually feel the way they do because of some factor in their background. The problem in any case is a spiritual one — such boys need Christ. He is the answer, and there is no boy anywhere for whose problem He is inadequate.

Other boys hinder the meeting because of personality or character traits or lacks resulting from poor training and inadequate homes. They literally don't seem to know how to behave, or because of some frustrated desire for attention or recognition, they tend to misbehave for the very sake of the attention they can attract.

However, the greatest reason for boys' misbehavior in club meetings is a program problem. The program fails to adequately challenge the full interests of fellows because it is poorly planned or poorly led, and hence they give their attention to other activities.

Discipline problems must be met both collectively and individually. The leader's most immediate need is for the control of the group as such, although basically every question of discipline is an individual one, and fair dealing requires that it be reckoned as such.

Group discipline to be effective is almost entirely a positive thing. The key to the success in it is to keep the gang's code of acceptance aimed in the right direction. These three rules will help.

(1) *Expect cooperation.* Remember that a boy desires his leader's confidence. Your expectation of the right sort of behavior from the group will do much to produce it. Act and think as though the normal thing is perfect behavior. A necessary addition to this is the next rule.

(2) *Require good order.* Don't overlook little disorders just because they don't bother you much. Deal with them quickly, firmly, and pleasantly, without interrupting the program. Don't allow fellows to think they are getting away with things they themselves recognize to be wrong. If little disturbances are quelled, big ones will be avoided.

(3) *Use Junior Leadership.* From your whole gang you have chosen out these fellows who in most cases have the largest influence over the opinion of the gang. You and they are working together, and they are as vitally concerned as you are with the success, and therefore the order, of the Battalion meeting. Give Corporals authority to enforce order within their Squads, and stand behind them fully. These leaders, who might be the most likely ones to be causing trouble if they had no responsibility, are your most powerful force for order.

Occasionally, of course, you must come up against the problem of what to do if the junior leaders themselves don't cooperate. In talking to a Corporal or Sergeant who has fallen short of your standard of expectation, you have an especially strong factor for helping him to see the seriousness of his failure, namely, he ought to realize that the offence is greater by virtue of the very fact that he is a leader. His need is for a deeper appreciation of leadership responsibility. If, however, he is unwilling to accept it, he doesn't deserve to be a leader.

INDIVIDUAL DISCIPLINE

In the final analysis individual discipline underlies all group control. Again it is important to differentiate between positive and negative discipline. Positive discipline says,"Let's do this," and motivates to right action, whereas negative discipline says "Don't do that," and corrects wrong action. Both are necessary in combination, but positive discipline should come first.

Positive discipline is accomplished by holding up before the boy high standards of behavior, *expecting* him to meet them, being genuinely surprised if he fails. This represents presenting a challenge to the fellow to live up to your trust. Remembering that discipline means training, your holding a boy to those standards which he has recognized as right helps him to build moral strength of character.

Discipline which does not help a fellow to develop self-discipline is not accomplishing its purpose. The quality of personal fortitude or self-control, variously described as stamina, backbone, strength of character, — and popularly as "guts," "spyzseringctum" or ability to "take it," — is one of the most important character traits for a boy to develop under your leadership. The basic quality is self-discipline. A vital part of self-discipline is self-judgment, that is, getting a fellow to see the situation and pass judgment on it himself. Boys as a whole, when faced squarely with a proposition like this, are willing to frankly evaluate their wrong and even subscribe the rightful punishment. The basis for putting the judgment up to a boy himself is that he himself knows better than anyone else whether the thing he did was wrong or not. If it was wrong, he knows also what is just in the treatment of it.

Punishment is by no means to be considered as a necessity under all circumstances. But the matter should be dealt with fairly, simply, and without unnecessary delay in such a manner that the boy himself feels afterward that he had a fair deal; that he was not dealt with harshly, on the one hand, or "got away with something" on the other.

PUNISHMENT

A complete picture of discipline carries with it the factor of punishment. There can be no effective training if infractions of the rules are not dealt with. Even nature has its penalties, as anyone who has eaten green apples well knows!

The purpose of punishment is to establish and make clear and certain to the boy effected and to anyone else who might be involved the fact of the individual's responsibility to the group.

As already noted, a fellow's self-judgment plays a large part in discipline. In punishment, a good deal of your work is accomplished when the fellow realizes the justice of the penalty. To achieve that, a number of things must be considered.

The conditions under which the punishment is given are all-impor tant. Never punish in anger. If a boy feels he is "getting it" because of his leader's lack of self control rather than because of his own wrong doing, he not only loses respect for his leader but also has occasion to brood over supposed injustice. The leader's object is not the soothing of his personal feelings, but rather the training of the boy.

Then, judgment must be used in the publicity of the punishment. A minor misdeed punished openly before the gang may humiliate a sensitive fellow to the place where he leaves the group. On the other hand, a public penalty may be just the thing for a "smart-alec" type of fellow who will be put in his place and profit by the experience. The leader must judge the circumstances.

Finally, there is the form of the punishment. Among other things the penalty should never be such as to reflect upon the honorableness of any certain job or duty. At a certain camp, for instance, dishwashing had been a fairly acceptable job. It was something that had to be done as part of a camp. Then one day a certain leader, violently displeased with the actions of one of the boys, loudly proclaimed, "If you do that again, you'll wash the dishes all day tomorrow!" Before the day was over, dishwashing had become a distasteful job. There was a stigma attached to it now; it was a penalty.

Having to sit out a game, being barred from special activity, and penalties of that nature will usually prove effective in the Battalion. Some leaders will find a demerit system usable. In some cases a "paddle-machine" (the offender swatted as he crawl through legs of the fellows or goes down the line) can be handy.

Remember again, that punishment, like discipline in general, should sometimes be strict, always firm and kind.

Leadership

Leadership is a normal part of a fellow's growth in Christ. Some fellows are outstanding in their natural leadership ability and it needs only direction and training. Many others need to have their ability to lead developed, because every normal adult will have some sphere in which he is required to assume certain leadership.

One very obvious way to tell a real leader is by the fact that he leads. Some fellows take natural leadership whenever they are with others, regardless of whether there is any program or plan involved. For your own thinking, as well as for talking with boys about leadership responsibility, here are four characteristics by which you can recognize the leader. Each is involved in the very idea of leadership.

1. *Being ahead.* A fellow cannot lead from behind.
2. *Moving.* A fellow cannot lead standing still.
3. *Being followed.* He who has no followers isn't leading.
4. *Going someplace.* Leading people requires leading them somewhere.

The *how* of your work in training junior leaders follows the three aspects of spiritual training, training in teamwork, and program training.

a. *Spiritual training.* In Brigade Achievement's guided study of the Word, biography of Christian pioneers, special Brigade leadership projects, and the correlation of spiritual things with the activities of everyday life, are provided effective channels of spiritual training for leadership.

b. *Training in teamwork.* This is perhaps the most distinctive phase of the Brigade leadership training program. The fellowship between non-coms in the Battalion, between junior leaders in camp, and between the members of Brigade Gospel teams is a potent force in character development.

c. *Program training.* Indoctrination into a particular work is the third important phase of leader training.

Thus, Battalion Sergeants will need to understand thoroughly their duties. For this the Squad section in the manual provides the necessary material, and the Captain will do well to drill and test on it extensively. Corporals likewise have their section for study. Because he is in close contact with the fellows through leadership of the Squad, the Corporal will come to you concerning discipline, Achievement stimulation, and other problems.

The opportunity to join with their Captain and Lieutenants in the planning and discussion of the meetings will in itself be a tremendous boost in leadership training.

Looking Ahead

Life, to a Christian fellow, as he stands in his school years looking ahead, is quite a different proposition than it is to a boy outside of Christ. For the non-Christian it is filled with dangers and uncertainties. For the Christian, these dangers and uncertainties become items in which he can have victory through his Lord. To the worldling life represents a series of choices based mostly on luck and guesswork. The Christian facing a similar series of equally challenging choices, relies not on guesswork, but seeking God's will; not on luck, but faith in God

Your first job in guiding your boys in looking ahead is to get that fact of confidence in God's leading itself across.

As he views the opening vistas of the years now stretching ahead of him, there are certain guide-posts that you will want to help a boy to find, principally the relation of the Word to his life decisions, and how to find the will of God. The two work together, for in the Word are all the changeless truths by which he can chart his course. Then, in prayer he must learn to take each decision of his life to the Lord.

He must ask Him for light on the decision to be made and then for grace to eliminate entirely the selfish motives.

Thus, as you see boys — boys whom you have guided — go out into life as Christian men with a testimony still "bright and keen for Christ," yours will indeed be the joy of a worker whose job for his Lord has been well done.

Appendix

NOTE: While a complete revision of the manual was not practical at the time of this printing, certain sections have been brought up-to-date with the 1955 Stockade program revision. Therefore, it has been necessary to extend some sections beyond the body of the text, concluding them in this brief appendix.

(continued from page 49)

5. *Brigade Lore.* In the Builder rank this includes the Brigade Motto, Stockade Song, and Stockade Benediction. Each Stockader should know these well and understand their meaning.

6. *National Flag.* In *Blockhouses* 3 and 4 there are brief sections on flag knowledge. In checking boys on these items, use suggested questions wherever they are given.

The first four *Blockhouses* are done in order. After these have been completed, the boy may go on to achieve the *Outposts* in whatever order he desires. Work on one *Blockhouse* unit should be completed before beginning another.

Stockade Sentinel (LOG, pp. 88-157)

The Sentinel section follows the same basic pattern as outlined for the Stockade Builder. The individual Achievement units are called *Stations*. The Stockade Sentinel rank is, of course, more advanced than the Builder rank, and there is a somewhat different approach to much of the Achievement work. In the stories, for instance, the Sentinel rank presents Christian missionary heroes such as Livingstone and Brainerd, thus introducing a missionary challenge.

No boy should begin the Sentinel work until he has reached the age of ten. Likewise, the boy who comes into the Stockade when he is ten or eleven should begin with the Sentinel Achievement. The Sentinel program has been carefully planned so that the essential elements from the Builder rank are incorporated, although perhaps in different form and on Sentinel level. It is not necessary or recommended, therefore, that a boy of the Sentinel age group start with the Builder rank for preliminary material.

After completing the first four *Stations* to earn the Sentinel rank pin, the boy may go on (as in the Builder rank) to achieve the *Outposts*. When he is at least 11½ years old and has earned the Sentinel rank pin, the Stockader may work toward the *Battalion Observer* award. This step will acquaint him with the Battalion program and prepare him for joining the Battalion when he becomes twelve.

Achievement Records

The STOCKADER'S LOG has been so planned that the boy's Achievement record is kept in his manual. There is a record chart at the end of each *Blockhouse* and *Station* as well as master records for both Builder and Sentinel ranks. The Handyman and Action Storehouses provide supplementary records.

All Achievement records in a boy's LOG should be entered by the leader *as soon as they are done*. Besides these entries, units of Achievement are recorded on the Notch-stick (refer to special sheet of Roster information for details). Also, the leader should keep his own record of each boy's progress. Thus, if a boy loses his book, the leader will have a duplicate record of what has been done.

(continued from page 103)

encourage Post loyalty. The boys should be proud of their own Post and strive to make it the best in the Stockade.

D. *Stockade Honors.* Following Post meetings, again the call, *"Build the Stockade,"* is given. This time the Compass Circle formation is used. (At the first few meetings it would be well for the Chief Ranger to add *"Compass Circle"* to the call.) As in the previous formation, success is achieved as the Rangers lead in it.

When the Stockade is formed in a circle, the Chief Ranger stands in the middle and gives the call, *"Dispatch."* He then faces the North Post and says, *"North."* The North Post Lookout steps forward and gives him the North Post meeting report. The same is done for each Post: North, East, South, and West in order. One of the Rangers quickly checks the reports and determines the Honor Post for that meeting. (Brigade Headquarters provides the "Honor Post Check Form" for this purpose.) The Honor Banner is attached to the Post Banner of the winning Post with appropriate ceremony. This is also the time when any Blockhouse or Station awards earned during that meeting are awarded.

Once each month the Honors time is an extra special affair. New Lookouts and Couriers are appointed to replace present ones. Also, this is the time when notches for Blockhouses or Stations achieved during the month are put on the Notch-sticks. If a rank has been completed during the month, the rank pin is awarded. This should be an impressive award ceremony, both to spur on Achievement work and also to be a high spot in the month of Stockade activity.

It may be necessary to shorten the Post meeting period on this night to allow extra Honors time. Parents may be invited for this Achievement recognition, too.

E. *Stockade Story Time.* Generally, the planning and presentation of the Stockade Story Time follows the principles set forth in the discussion on Battalion Council Ring (pp. 86-93 of this manual). In the Stockade, however, the main presentation is in story form and talks or discussions are used only infrequently. Singing, brief testimonies, flannelgraph, and reciting favorite Scripture verses all have a place in keeping this period varied and interesting.

Remember to prepare carefully for the spiritual challenge which this period usually affords. On the other hand, do not make this an extended evangelistic presentation. It is much better to use the Achievement program and other opportunities in the meeting for working with a boy personally, than to rely on Story Time alone for your spiritual work with boys.

F. *Dismissal.* Close your Stockade meeting promptly. Except in cases of personal dealing with a boy, every Stockader should be taught to leave for home immediately after the meeting is dismissed. Usually the Stockade Benediction is repeated to close the meeting.

*   *   *   *   *

It will be noted that the Stockade meeting has a certain amount of form and ceremony that at first may seem difficult to master. However, it follows a fairly simple pattern that can be learned easily, and once it is understood, follows along naturally. For instance, the opening of the meeting is simply getting boys into the proper formation, having prayer, and presenting colors. Such calls as "Stockade, *silence,*" are just the logical way of getting this accomplished.

Again, it is recommended that the leaders conduct a "practice" meeting, without the boys present, to familiarize themselves with the formations and calls. If it is done right the first few times, it will be easy to keep on doing it right!

Index

BRIGADE TRAILS

SUPPLEMENT
TO THE
LEADER'S
MANUAL

The material in this supplement
replaces most of the chapter on
Battalion achievement in the
Leader's Manual, pages 50-67.
It has been especially prepared for
use with Brigade Trails, Battalion
program manual, 8th edition
(1958), formerly known as
The Boy's Guidebook.

BRIGADE TRAILS ACHIEVEMENT

Brigade Trails is a revision and expansion of *The Boy's Guidebook*, 7th edition (1945). There are two basic divisions to the manual: *Adventure Trails*, for boys 12-14, and *Frontier Trails*, for boys 15-18. Each section has been prepared with careful attention to the interests, abilities and needs of the two age groups.

The Adventure Trails offer a progressive, well-rounded system of achievement and activity for the early adolescent boy as he advances through the ranks of Observer, Explorer, Trailblazer and Guide. The Frontier Trails open up much broader achievement opportunities along with their increasing stress upon leadership development and practical service.

The clear purpose of Brigade achievement is to help boys attain exceptional Christian maturity and leadership capabilities while they are developing natural skills and interests. The Herald of Christ award is the immediate goal of all achievement progress; each step in the program should have this end in view.

ADVENTURE TRAILS

In order to have a clear understanding of Adventure Trails achievement, a careful review of the program as presented in *Brigade Trails*, pages 13-111, is essential. After gaining a thorough knowledge of this section, the following discussions of each rank will help the leader understand and appreciate the most important features.

OBSERVER

The Observer is the introductory rank for boys just entering the Battalion. Its aim is to get boys started in the achievement program at once while they are becoming acquainted in the Battalion. The eight Observer steps combine natural interest features, basic Brigade lore and elementary study of the Bible:

1. Battalion membership is the first step and may already have been obtained (as outlined at the bottom of page 7).

2. The Brigade Code Drill—six silent hand signals—has a natural appeal for a boy of twelve.

3. The Tests of Strength provide a ready challenge for growing boys who are eager to demonstrate their physical abilities.

4. The Brigade Salute stresses basic Battalion courtesy and respect. It is important to realize at this point that the use of certain military forms and terminology have only a functional purpose and are not intended to parallel all the requirements of military usage.

5. The first three chapters of the Gospel of John place a boy in immediate contact with a vital area of Scripture. For some boys this may be the very first acquaintance with God's Word. As stressed on page 16, careful, intelligent reading is the foremost aim of Bible study for this age.

6. The Observer's Verse, John 3:16, is one of the greatest texts of all Scripture and an important starting point for a Scripture memory program.

7. The Brigade Motto, "Bright and Keen for Christ," has a central place in the program; it should be made very meaningful to every boy in Brigade, although it may not be fully comprehended at first.

8. As indicated, the Watchword is the Brigadier's benediction and is often used at the close of the meeting.

Observer requirements are obviously not difficult, and with encouragement a boy can easily meet them during the first several weeks of his attendance. It is important for a boy to realize that these requirements already constitute a start on Explorer achievement (e.g., the Tests of Strength; Bible reading). He should be given every encouragement to continue his progress without delay in order to achieve the Explorer rank as soon as possible.

Every effort should be made to determine a boy's spiritual background as soon as he enters the group. However it is best to avoid "pressuring" a decision for salvation until the Gospel has been clearly presented. The true meaning of what God has done for us as explained in John 3:16 should be clearly explained. The boy may respond openly to an invitation to receive Christ at his first opportunity. If he does not, there will be many other opportunities to reach him for Christ as he continues to be active in the program.

EXPLORER

The Explorer rank should be a continuation—without delay—following Observer recognition. There are four main steps to Explorer achievement:

1. *Explorer's Check Up.* This grouping of individual requirements includes: (a) Tests of Strength—natural physical challenges; (b) Brigade Know-How —items of lore and procedure; (c) Captain's Check—a chance for personal counsel with the leader.

The Captain's Check provides a natural opening for dealing with a boy's spiritual needs as *he comes to the leader* to explain the meaning of the Brigade Motto. The leader is in the unique position of not having the barrier between himself and the boy which ordinarily comes when a man "buttonholes" a boy to talk about spiritual things. The opportunity for spiritual guidance is above all other things, natural and unforced.

2. *Exploring the Outdoors.* The Explorer's hike can become a real hi-light activity for new fellows in the Battalion. If adult leaders join the hikes occasionally, they provide informal opportunities for getting better acquainted with boys.

3. *Exploring the Word of God.* This requirement is well explained on pages 22 and 23 of *Brigade Trails.* The emphasis at this stage is regular, careful reading with comprehension. Although a chapter-a-day is not definitely required, it is encouraged to help establish the habit of daily reading. A significant spiritual truth is emphasized to unsaved and Christian fellows alike when they mark the word "believe" wherever it occurs. The Explorer's Verse, John 1:10-12, is one of the best passages in the Bible for leading a boy to accept the Lord Jesus Christ as his personal Saviour. As a boy comes to his leader to recite the passage, it is natural for the leader to ask, "Do you understand what those verses mean . . . can you tell me the name of one person who did receive Him and became a son of God?" In this connection, "How to Believe" (page 25) may help both the leader and the boy to understand the simplicity and reality of faith in Christ.

4. *Exploring in Sports and Crafts.* The Reference Section lists a variety of skills and activities for boys 12-14 (pages 69 and 75). They are preliminary to the more developed Frontier Trails craft standards for older boys. Although a boy ought to show adequate proficiency in the activity or subject of his choice, this is not the age for a high degree of specialization. As in the testing of all other achievement, the leader should require a boy to meet a standard equal to his level of maturity and fair to other members of the group.

TRAILBLAZER

The Trailblazer rank marks an important step ahead in a boy's achievement progress. In addition to exploring new trails of adventure, he begins to mark a trail for others to follow. There are five major parts to this rank:

1. *Trailblazer's Check Up.* This parallels the Explorer Check Up with its grouping of requirements. Elements of Brigade lore and drill are again introduced. Most important of these is the Captain's Check on the Seven Points of Valor. Refer to the *Leader's Manual* pages 51 and 52, for a helpful discussion of these. Keep in mind, however, that the last point is now known as *Dedication*—the complete surrender of oneself to God for His service and use.

2. *Your Trailmate.* This characteristic phase of Brigade—"bring a buddy" —includes both inviting a newcomer to the Battalion and helping him get started in the Observer rank. Normally, trailmates are in the same Squad and the instruction of the Observer takes place during the Squad meeting. In situations where enlisting new members would be extremely difficult to fulfill, the leader may suggest an alternative requirement which involves leading or helping others.

3. *Bible Adventure Trails.* Following the Explorer's reading of the Gospel of John, the Trailblazer candidate begins a progressive study of the New Testament. Reading through the Gospel of Luke and Acts 1-12 provides a continuous narrative for the life of Christ and the establishment of the early church. Pages 36 and 37 provide questions to stimulate thought and encourage a more careful reading of the books. These questions are not intended to be used for an "examination" of the boy's knowledge by his leader, however, for it is the careful, thoughtful reading of the Scripture which is important. The leader should be alert to answer any difficulties which may have been encountered during the reading. In addition to the reading, more key verses have been selected for memorization.

4. *Outdoor Trails.* This requirement combines achievement progress with activities of especially high boy-interest. Planned Battalion outings provide opportunities for passing requirements such as this while sparking general interest in the group.

5. *Trails in Sports and Crafts.* This is similar to the sports and crafts requirement in the Explorer rank, except that one of each must be earned. The leader should provide counsel in the choice of these subjects whenever it seems natural or is desired. A higher degree of ability may be expected from boys as their maturity increases.

GUIDE

The boy has made commendable progress in achievement by this point, and he has probably had opportunity to develop leadership ability as a Lance Corporal or Corporal of a Squad. He continues to learn and develop his abilities in the Guide rank while he begins to have a greater concern for others as he assumes a place of leadership among them. The Guide rank broadens to include six main steps:

1. *Guide's Check Up.* This is similar to Explorer and Trailblazer Check Ups, but several choices are offered as tests of mental and physical strength. The complete Fifteen Points of Drill are required here, although several were introduced previously. The Story of Brigade will give the boy an insight into the history and scope of the organization of which he is a member. He should be able to retell the general pattern of development in his own words, mentioning significant points.

The Captain's Check on the understanding of the Brigadier's Purpose gives the leader one of his best opportunities to talk with the individual boy about his relationship to Christ. It is normal for a boy already to have received Christ as Saviour at this stage of his advancement, but this may not be true for every Brigadier. Through this requirement the boy comes to the leader to explain to him the way of salvation. It is not necessarily true that a boy must profess acceptance of Christ as his Saviour to pass the test, but he should show an understanding of the way of salvation. The leader talks with him alone and makes sure that he knows. It gives the leader an opportunity to find out where the boy stands personally, and he has a natural chance to lead an unsaved boy to Christ. It is very important, however, to avoid giving any boy the idea that the acceptance of Christ is a mechanical thing or part of a test to be passed.

For those who have received Christ as Saviour, the Brigadier's Purpose becomes an expression of the desire to live a sincere Christian life, and the Captain's Check affords another opportunity for counsel in Christian growth.

2. *Guiding in the Battalion.* If leadership opportunity has not been provided, it is offered at this point. Reading the *Noncom's Handbook* gives the proper information for Squad leadership; actual experience—with proper supervision—makes this an important phase of leadership development.

3. *Guideposts in God's Word.* The Guide's Bible study takes up the missionary career of Paul (Acts 13-28) and his epistles. One of the books is to be studied in a systematic way according to the outline on page 53. Important memory verses have been selected from the reading. The Guide's Verse, II Timothy 2:1-4, is a passage of tremendous challenge to young fellows who are training to serve Christ.

4. *Great Missionary Guides.* An acquaintance with great missionary heroes is especially important when a boy is developing his own character and leadership potential. The study of the lives of such pioneers has inspired many boys to dedicate their lives to the Lord for missionary service. The brief biographies presented in the manual offer a glimpse at some of the outstanding personalities. The local church should provide a library of more complete missionary biographies for boys or at least know where they may be obtained. As a leader you should read some of these books yourself, for they will give you a vision for your own work as well as provide a vast source of story material for Council Ring. When a boy comes to be approved on his reading, encourage him to check over his own life as to the qualifications for doing pioneer work for God on the foreign or home mission field.

5. *Guide's Wilderness Expedition.* This outdoor activity allows for considerable originality on the part of both leader and boys. The expeditions can be taken during the course of a Battalion or Squad hike. The excitement of the adventurous situations may stimulate the progress of other boys who have not advanced as far as the candidates for this test and who must stay at the base while the expeditions are in operation.

6. *Sports and Crafts for Guides.* In addition to completing requirements for one sports and one crafts project, the boy is introduced to the Frontier Trails crafts in some subject of his interest. He may earn a "certificate" from any of the standards listed in the back of the manual. If he has not already done so, the boy may be encouraged to look over the Frontier Trails program and begin to determine his course of advancement following Guide recognition.

FRONTIER TRAILS

The door of page 113 opens a new approach to Brigade achievement for the boy of Guide rank. Seven "trails" of specialized achievement are offered—Airman, Craftsman, Landsman, Mariner, Sportsman, Technician, Woodsman. A boy must choose one of these trails and follow it through a three-stage advancement program. Upon completion of "Three Star" requirements, he becomes a candidate for the Herald of Christ award, Brigade's highest achievement recognition. In addition to the objective Herald of Christ standards, he must demonstrate all-around Christian character and leadership ability.

FOR GUIDES ONLY

Under normal circumstances a boy enters the Frontier Trails program during his fourteenth or fifteenth year after he has completed the ranks of Observer, Explorer, Trailblazer and Guide. Most boys will enter the Battalion at twelve or thirteen, when they are best suited for Adventure Trails achievement levels. They should be encouraged to begin achieving immediately and be given every possible opportunity to make steady progress toward entrance to the Frontier Trails at fifteen. Rarely does a boy earn the Guide rank before he is fourteen, but Guide status is the only basic requirement for entering the Frontier Trails.

An Older Boy Joins the Battalion

Occasionally the leader faces the situation of a boy entering the Battalion as a new member at the age of fifteen or older. The boy may or may not be mature and well adjusted for his age; he may or may not be a Christian. Yet the Brigade Battalion has much to offer him if his interest continues and he enters wholeheartedly into the achievement program and activities.

Two basic suggestions are offered to meet this situation: (1) have the boy enter the Adventure Trails program at the Observer level and earn each successive rank while at the same time beginning Frontier Trails achievement with other boys of his age; or, (2) permit him to by-pass certain Adventure Trails requirements, earning only Guide recognition, while also beginning Frontier Trails achievement. Either of these alternatives will be influenced by such factors as the number of other boys his age in the Battalion and the level of their achievement progress.

The first of the two suggestions may appear to be the easiest and the fairest to younger boys, but it may result in a loss of interest on the part of the older boy and eventual loss of the boy himself to the Battalion. It would be better to have him miss some of the Adventure Trails experiences than to drop out entirely after a few tries at the Explorer rank. Even though this may seem to be the best solution, follow it with caution, for some boys may eagerly try to earn all possible recognition while others are content to achieve basic requirements in order to keep up with the activities and interests of others their own age.

The second possibility should be a matter for the leader's own judgment; it is nowhere mentioned in the boy's manual. If chosen, it should include the following: (1) earn the Guide rank as outlined in the Adventure Trails; (2) complete the following additional requirements: (a) learn the Brigade Hymn, Motto, Watchword and Seven Points of Valor; (b) read the Gospel of John, Luke and Acts 1-12. Guide recognition only would be awarded for this achievement. The leader must determine at what age to permit this exception, but rarely should it be made for a boy under fifteen and under no circumstance for boys who have obviously been "stalling" to avoid some of the Adventure Trails requirements.

In any event, get the older boy started in the Frontier Trails program where requirements are geared to his level of physical and mental development, for an active interest here will be the best possible stimulus to his total achievement. Recognition for progress in the Frontier Trails should be reserved until after the Guide rank has been achieved. When an older boy is obviously unsaved or lacks an understanding of spiritual things, counsel more closely with him and carefully supervise his opportunities to lead and influence others (e.g., leading Squad meetings as required for the Guide rank).

UNDERSTANDING FRONTIER TRAILS ACHIEVEMENT

A thorough understanding of the content of the Frontier Trails is essential to effective leadership in this program. Although the leader need not be a skilled specialist in any or all of the seven specialized trails, he should be familiar with the basic structure and aims as outlined on pages 115-191.

While each of the seven trails may be analyzed for its own distinctive elements, there are important similarities which all share alike. The following points should be noted:

1. Each trail follows a progressive one, two and three step system of advancement.

2. Each of the three steps (or "Stars") consists of eight requirements. Half of the eight are identical for all other trails (e.g., compare One Star Airman requirements with One Star Craftsman, etc.).

3. Each trail begins with broad, general achievement and progresses toward more detailed and specialized interests. No trail attempts to provide complete technical training in its field.

4. Each trail seeks to relate itself to positive opportunities for Christian leadership and service (e.g., missionary service opportunities) wherever this is natural or unforced. Such emphasis is also well supplemented by the variety of practical service projects included in the Frontier Trails program.

5. Each trail is similarly presented in the manual with no attempt to value one achievement choice above another.

The identical elements for all trails such as Bible reading, doctrine study, service projects and crafts deserve additional consideration.

Bible Reading and Scripture Memory

Pages 177 and 178 list the requirements for One, Two and Three Star and Herald of Christ ranks. The schedule includes completing the reading of the New Testament (Matthew, Mark, James—Revelation) and reading through most of the Old Testament. The Psalms are suggested as part of daily devotional reading. The Bible survey booklets (ETTA) mentioned on page 178 are highly recommended as guides for introductory Bible study. They are available through Brigade Headquarters Supply Department.

The Bible memorization program consists of selected verses building upon what was already achieved in the Adventure Trails. Certain verses parallel the doctrine study required for the particular rank.

Bible Doctrine Study

The doctrine study requirements are presented on pages 179-183. Since these studies are especially worthwhile and involve concepts which are often difficult to grasp, boys working in this area need the best possible counseling. If the pastor or some qualified person other than the regular Battalion leadership guides boys in these studies, he should have an acquaintance with the entire achievement program and its aims. It is especially important for those who do not regularly test achievement progress to know what may be expected of a boy. The counselor should avoid making requirements too strict —the Brigade program does not attempt to provide a "Bible school education" in these subjects.

Two texts have been especially recommended for reference in studying the doctrines. The ETTA manuals are available through Brigade Headquarters Supply Department. Some other text may be preferred by your pastor which presents the official teaching of your denomination or individual church.

Service Projects

The leadership and service projects provide a practical expression for an older boy's desire to do something useful with his abilities and energy. Moreover, they offer Brigade achievement recognition to those who are already actively serving in the Battalion, in the Church, in school or in the community. To avoid misuse of this double recognition possibility, these activities should be reviewed carefully by the leader. Projects for which credit is granted should promote worthwhile, Christ-honoring activities with a clear purpose behind them. The boy should be encouraged to choose a variety of activities so that all of his service units are not earned in one project that is repeated. Achievement credit should seldom be granted for experiences which took place while the boy was working in the Adventure Trails.

Craft Achievement

The list of standards which begins on page 192 contains requirements for eighty-six different subjects. As indicated, there are two levels of achievement for many of the subjects. Wherever it is practical or helpful, Brigade achievement credit is given upon evidence of satisfactory school work in the craft subject or training provided by some other recognized agency such as the American Red Cross (for first aid and water safety), the National Rifle Association for riflery and hunting), etc. Helpful literature available from other organizations, such as the Civil Air Patrol booklets mentioned for aviation crafts, has also been suggested.

Refer to the discussion in the *Leader's Manual*, pages 65-67, for suggestions on the matter of crafts in the Brigade program, keeping in mind the changes made in the 8th edition of the boy's manual. While boys should be encouraged to earn a wide variety of craft certificates as required in the Frontier Trails program, leaders should direct all achievement progress toward the main goal of regular advancement in the ranks. Crafts provide only one aspect of a boy's training while the full program of each rank meets other vital needs.

GUIDING BOYS THROUGH FRONTIER TRAILS

Boys may enter upon the Frontier Trails singly, advancing at their own initiative, or they may form a special group working together on a trail. Sometimes this group will be an already organized Squad, or it may be a club made up of boys from several Squads. It is normally best for the fellows to remain directly associated with the Battalion, because of the need for their leadership and, in turn, their need for leadership opportunity.

Extra meetings of these Frontier Trails Squads or clubs can be held by the Captain, Lieutenant or other similarly qualified person who has ability in the trail being followed. Since craft requirements and rank requirements are parallel for some trails, well-qualified craft guides may also serve as trail advisors (the suggestions regarding craft guides in the *Leader's Manual*, pages 65-67, may be re-applied here). In some localities boys from several Battalions who share similar interests may join together to work on Frontier Trails achievement under the guidance of adult leadership chosen from the area.

HERALD OF CHRIST

The Herald of Christ rank is the acme of Brigade achievement. This top rank however does not represent a final pinnacle from which every step must be downward, but rather the state of being full grown as a Brigadier. The Herald has not reached the end of his opportunity for advancement, for ahead of him stretch great and challenging vistas of leadership and service.

The content of Herald requirements is primarily of the sort to test leadership development and maturity in the Christian life. Having come thus far through attainment of the various steps of progress in Brigade, the boy has learned to correlate his full round of activities with the things of the Lord and of His word. No longer is he being tested primarily in individual activities, but rather on the sum total of what all of these activities have contributed to his spiritual strength and to his usefulness as a servant of Christ. The following information will aid in the understand of the detail requirements.

1. *Brigade Leadership.* Besides continued participation in local Brigade activities, the Herald of Christ candidate is asked to complete the C.S.B. adult leader training program. This will prepare him for continued Brigade participation on an adult level as well as supplement his leadership growth.

2. *Christian Character.* This is perhaps the most subjective requirement in all of the Brigade program, for it is more than anything else a measure of *quality.* It must be remembered that the Herald of Christ rank does not require "perfection," but rather stresses positive maturity of Christian growth. Rarely would a boy be held back by this requirement if he has had proper counsel in previous advancement. The written theme allows an opportunity for expression of beliefs and principles which are the result of his spiritual development.

3. *Study of God's Word.* This requirement continues in the pattern of previous Frontier Trails ranks.

4. *Practical Service.* Additional service projects help give expression to leadership growth.

5. *C.S.B. Approval.* Personal contact with a Brigade Headquarters approved representative supplements local approval and assures a high standard of achievement for all Herald candidates.

BATTALION MEETING PROCEDURE

The local club meeting remains essentially as outlined in the *Leader's Manual,* Chapter Six (page 69 ff.). It may be found helpful in the established Battalion to allow more time for Squad meetings and the "Captain's Special." A twenty minute Squad meeting will permit greater concentration on achievement, provided there is active participation and enthusiasm in this phase of the program. Occasional lengthening of the Captain's Special will be worthwhile for craft and achievement demonstrations, instructional films, etc. This program feature should maintain its "variety" aspects, however. Extra time which may have been allowed for these periods may be borrowed from the game period or result in a longer meeting. In any event, move quickly from one part of the program to another without time lags; avoid lengthy meetings when a better planned one could have been shorter.

It has already been suggested that considerable Frontier Trails enthusiasm may encourage separate sessions for older boys in addition to the regular Battalion meeting. It would involve an informal type of meeting plan with a majority of the time set aside to study and discuss their particular interests together.

ADJUSTMENT TO THE EIGHTH EDITION

For groups which have been active prior to the release of *Brigade Trails*, there is a temporary adjustment from the program of the *Boy's Guidebook*, 7th edition. The method of adjustment is largely up to the Captain of each local Battalion who best understands the individual boys, their present achievement progress, and their abilities. The adjustment should be made as fair as possible to the individual boy, to others in the Battalion and to the high standards of the Brigade program. The following general principles should be considered by the Captain for the smoothest adjustment.

Adventure Trails

1. Ranks previously earned are considered equivalent to those in the 8th edition. It is unnecessary for a boy to earn "Observer" if the Explorer rank has been achieved or significantly started.

2. Where part of any rank has been earned, the boy may either: (a) complete it according to the 7th edition standards, (b) earn the rank based entirely on 8th edition requirements, or (c) transfer credit for comparable tests and complete the balance of needed achievement from 8th edition standards (e.g., the Health Chart is equivalent to the Tests of Strength; the reading of Mark is equivalent to the reading of John, etc.).

Frontier Trails

1. Previous Airman, Mariner or Woodsman achievement may generally be accepted. However, any 8th edition requirements which have been bypassed should be reviewed and an attempt made to complete them wherever possible. New manual standards should be followed for any further achievement.

2. Previous Ranger achievement may be completed under old standards or adapted to one of the seven trails of the new manual.

3. All Herald of Christ achievement should be based upon 8th edition standards.

CPSIA information can be obtained at www.ICGtesting.com
Printed in the USA
LVOW01s0047230915

455359LV00037B/994/P